NO MATTER WATT!

The Recipe to a 7-Figure Income in Sales

By

Michael O'Donnell

This book is dedicated to my lovely wife Marcia,

my sons Joseph and Erick and my daughter Katherine.

You mean everything to me.

Author Bio

Michael O'Donnell has been the number one salesman on planet earth in the rooftop solar industry for the last five years running. He has received not one but two of the highly coveted Golden Door awards in each of those years. He is a partner in and the Vice President of Sales and Marketing of SunSolar Solutions the largest solar sales and installation company in his home market of Arizona. He has been a keynote speaker at numerous conferences and industry summits. He is regularly featured on many podcasts and panels.

He and his wife Marcia have been clean and sober for over 38 years and are the parents of three college graduates. They live in a beautiful home in Peoria AZ. They enjoy spending time at their cabin in the Rim Country above Payson AZ.

Are you an undisciplined procrastinator suffering under the burden of recognizable talent and tremendous potential but ashamed of the meager, mediocre and unremarkable results that you've produced so far? If I could've got past my ego and stripped away the false narrative that I had carefully constructed, that's exactly how I would have described myself as I was turning 50 years old after a "successful" 25 year career in sales. This book is about the break throughs that led to a repeatable recipe for a seven figure income in sales and to becoming the number one solar salesperson in the world.

One noteworthy achievement I had accomplished was staying sober for over 30 years. I managed to do this by following the clear directions of some sage old timers who convinced me to make a sacred commitment to doing the most absurdly simple things every day, no matter what. Their wisdom and guidance gave me the ability to see how high the stakes were which gave me the strength and courage to avoid devastating consequences and walk a healthy, productive path.

After being thrust into the once-in-a-generation-opportunity of helping homeowners transition from expensive and destructive fossil fuels for their home energy needs to clean, green renewable and free solar power which helps them build wealth while solving the primary existential threat to our planet, I found myself in an genuine gold rush but heading for the same disappointing results.

A series of breakthroughs inspired me to create a sacred commitment to a handful of absurdly simple "No Matter Watt" daily behaviors. These combined with the ancient arts of prospecting, presenting and one-call closing taught to me by another group of sage old timers, have blessed me with legendary results, and an easy to follow, repeatable recipe for generating a seven figure income in sales.

This book will enable you to:

Forge a 9-figure mindset required to generate a 7-figure income

Overcome the inertia caused by the dread of rejection

Monetize the word NO and become the beneficiary of momentum

Get invited to the kitchen table or board room table in one conversation

Deliver a compelling presentation that lights the prospects ass on fire

Build a framework that explains why you are "not coming back"

Execute the today only close after being told "they need to think about it"

As actual talent and substantial potential are required to utilize these hacks, habits and skills, this book is not for everyone. However, if you are ready to take action and follow the directions of this recipe then pick up this book and let's begin the path to a seven figure income that's produced by a nine-figure mindset. You have the opportunity to throw off the golden handcuffs of the American Routine and set out on an adventure together to achieve generational wealth and the American Dream.

Table of Contents

Foreword 11

Introductions 13

Preface 19

Part 1: The Journey to a 7-Figure Income in Sales 25

Chapter 1: Birth of a Salesman 25

Chapter 2: First Things First: Kill What's Killing You 31

Chapter 3: Solar to the Rescue 38

Chapter 4: It Matters What You Sell and Who You Sell it For 51

Part 2: Create Your 9-Figure Mindset 57

Chapter 5: The Importance of a 9-Figure Mindset 57

Chapter 6: Create Your 9-Figure Morning 61

Chapter 7: Go For No: It's Where the Money Is 77

Part 3: 7-Figure Prospecting 88

Chapter 8: Making Appointments 88

Chapter 9: The Hacks and Magic of 7-Figure Prospecting 94

Chapter 10: How to Get a Yes on the Door: "I've Got to Go" 106

Part 4: The Compelling Presentation 117

Chapter 11: Make a Friend, Make a Sale 117

Chapter 12: Build the Door Frame 127

Chapter 13: Hang the Door—From Education to Understanding to Knowledge 134

Chapter 14: The Advanced Solar Presentation—The Four Big Things 141

Part 5: The 7-Figure Close 158

Chapter 15: Overcoming Objections...158

Chapter 16: The Master Closer Mindset..171

Chapter 17: Execution - Close the Door 183

Part 6: Following Up and a Call to Action..211

Chapter 18: The 7-Figure Follow Up..211

Chapter 19: Final Words and Resources 215

Foreword

Coach Micheal Burt
17X time author
#1 Activator of Prey Drive in the world
Former championship coach

I first met Michael O'Donnell at the D2DCon conference in Salt Lake City in 2019. I was giving a keynote address and he had just received not one but two golden door awards in Solar. He was introduced to me as the guy that literally did 2 1/2 times the volume of the very best in the industry. He has gone on to win not one but two of those Golden Door awards for five years in a row and is regularly called out as the GOAT of Solar. It's been my pleasure to spend many hours working together. He's been a keynote speaker at my Monster nation event.

It's become clear to me that Michael has an incredible breadth and depth about him. He reads ferociously, he studies intently, he invests in himself and his team, and he executes like no other. His confidence in his presentations and specifically in his conviction to close and convert is unmatched across anyone in his industry. Quickly after my beginning in some of my coaching, I named him the #1 face-to-face sales person in the world, not just in the door-to-door space. This is a tall feat.

Michael is hungry. He exhibits the habits of the top 1% of performers in the world. He has made a decision to go pro in life but more importantly, he is now in a season of transferring his knowledge, his skills, his desire, and his confidence to others.

This is legacy that will far transcend just his own production.

Enjoy and devour this book if you have a desire to be the best, not just someone in the field.

Introductions

Sam Taggart
Founder & CEO, D2Dexperts
Author of ABC'$ of Closing
Keynote Speaker

I am standing on the main stage at the first event D2DCon I hosted back in Jan 2018, giving an industry award away for the top one percent of all salespeople in each industry in the direct sales world. I was new to this MC job, and by all means, who really gave me any authority to make up some award at the time called the Golden Door?

We got to the solar industry, and I started calling up the individuals who had earned the requirements to get it, and all of a sudden, this "older" guy from the crowd shouts, "Wait a minute, I technically did two times that! Does that mean I get two awards?"

I, of course, reply, "Who the heck is this dude? And there is no way that is possible!"

He then goes on to validate his outstanding performance, and I bring him on stage to award the first ever Double Golden Door winner. From that day on, Michael has won a Double Golden Door each year for the past five years. This award has since become an industry standard that thousands of sales reps strive to obtain. Only around 20 or so each year accomplish this feat, and only a select few have ever earned a Double Golden Door.

One year, Tim Grover, the former personal trainer of Kobe Bryant, Michael Jordan, and other very high-level performers, came and spoke about his book and the concept of being relentless. He calls the cream of the crop "cleaners". These aren't people who win just one championship; they win back-to-back-to-back championships. "Cleaner" would be the best way to categorize Michael O'Donnell.

Since giving that award in 2018, I have had the privilege to work with Michael on a one-on-one coaching basis, and he has traveled the world with our mastermind group, Experts Circle. It's one thing to study the greats, observing them from afar, but to get to know the inner workings of how they operate on a regular basis and over a long period of time brings a whole new perspective on what puts someone in the top one percent in their field.

Michael has some distinct principles you can tell he has embodied and developed over the span of his sales career. The ones that have truly stood out to me are:

Discipline: He creates systems that he doesn't break in order to keep consistently prospecting, and he doesn't allow himself to get complacent.

Humility: Despite being one of the best in the industry, he invests meaningful money each year into coaching, conferences, masterminds, books, and more.

Habits: He has built a powerful relationship to consistency, doing the basics every day no matter the cost.

Faith: He has a strong relationship with God, and he looks for ways to make an impact and give back.

And lastly: *Leadership*. Michael for the longest time built his identity around being the best at sales. There was a defining moment at a retreat we hosted in Idaho where I had to kick him in the nuts for a second and help him realize that he had been playing selfish and impatient when it came to developing others. He has since reframed his mentality over the last few years, and it has been fun to watch him turn the spotlight off himself and onto the people he leads. He has started to see big growth in his company, and now his gifts can bless and change the lives of those in his influence. The reason why this book now exists is because he realized how much he has to offer the world; he just needed to find outlets through which to let his light shine!

I know that as you read this book, you will pull nuggets out that can not only make you a lot more money but, more importantly, create life-long habits that are applicable to any area of performance. By taking in the wisdom of a lifelong master of the sales game, you can shortcut your way to success and save yourself some dummy tax.

Brad Lea
Founder & Chairman, LightSpeed VT
Host of the Dropping Bombs Podcast
Author of The Hard Way
Lead Instructor of Closer School

I have a tremendous amount of respect for the sales people in the door-to-door sales world. I've done a lot of work with Sam Taggart over the years and I've been very happy to have my LightSpeed VT platform deliver the outcome changing content housed there for the D2D University.

I first became aware of Michael O'Donnell when his solar sales training started blowing up and creating so much traffic in the D2D University hosted on the LightSpeed VT platform. To be perfectly honest with you, I was somewhat skeptical about some of the counterintuitive things he was teaching, like going up to a door and trying to get the prospect to say no. I mean who teaches sales people to go out every day and find people to say no. I found out that the reason people were seeking out his training was that they were experiencing breakthroughs that were generating legendary results!

I had the pleasure of being the keynote speaker at D2Dcon in 2020 and saw a couple dozen people in the entire industry honored for selling over 1,000,000 watts of solar in a year and brought up to the stage to receive a Golden Door award. And then there was Michael O'Donnell brought up to the stage to receive not one but two Golden Door awards for having sold more than 2 1/2 million watts of solar for what was then the fourth year in a row. I started to get a glimpse of why so many sales people were benefiting so greatly by his training.

When my good friend Coach Micheal Burt called me to suggest that he and I meet with Michael about creating the MOD Sales Academy and have it join the Grant Cardone, Anthony Robbins and my Closers School training on LightSpeed VT, I told him we needed to get that moving as soon as possible and he and Micheal jumped on his jet to come meet with me in Las Vegas. We built a plan to develop the curriculum and started assembling a top tier team of my producers to bring that training to the market at lightspeed.

It just so happened that Legacy Patiño, one of my superstar project managers for training content development, was also an up-and-coming solar executive and had a solar sales team of his own in Las Vegas and Yuma Arizona. In addition to collaborating with Michael to transform his proven methods into the virtual training realm, he became completely convinced that this training would make the difference and could catapult his sales teams to a much higher level of success. In mid project development, he and his partner Cesar Delgadillo joined SunSolar Solutions, Michael's solar company in the southwest where their teams are now and generating a multi million dollar amount of solar sales every month!

I couldn't be more pleased with how that training has turned out or more excited with how many sales professionals have enrolled in the MOD Sales Academy in the short short time since it's been released. The mission of LightSpeed VT is to get the knowledge from the people who have it to the people who need it, is spectacularly validated by people who experience these kinds of results. The feedback coming from the sales professionals enrolled is astounding. I had one individual come up to me at an event and tell me, "I left my old industry and started selling solar after learning how lucrative it could be. In my whole first year I was able to sell six solar systems. Since being enrolled in the training six weeks ago I have sold 26 solar systems!"

Since our first meeting it's been a real pleasure to get to know Michael. We have had many in-depth conversations on my lakeside patio at my corporate headquarters and numerous dinners. He has been a guest trainer and has enthralled the students of my Closers School. We have shared the stage at D2DCon and Micheal Burt's Monster Nation conferences. He spoke at a seminar for roofers exploring the solar business at my conference venue here in Las Vegas where he stole the show and moved numerous companies to sign up for training programs that cost over $100,000.

I believe that the ideas and methods Michael will transmit to you both in this book and in the companion MOD Sales Academy, can propel you to the highest level of success in your sales career and quickly enable you to experience the 7 Figure income results you are seeking.

Preface

My story is very different from those of most people who sell books about sales. I have never been in the business of selling sales training. After selling 1 million watts (1 megawatt or 1 MW) in my first year back selling solar and 2.5 MW in my second year, I came to my first D2DCon and was brought to the stage to receive a Golden Door Award.

Sam Taggart, the CEO of D2D Experts and master of ceremonies of D2DCon, told me the award was for reaching the pinnacle of achievement in solar sales, which was 1 million watts of solar power sold in one year. No one had ever contemplated selling 2 million, let alone 2.5 million, watts in one year. After telling me he didn't have an award for that, he brought me to the stage that night and handed me two trophies. That was the birth of the Double Golden Door Award. I have sold between 2 and 3 MW of solar power every year since and have received two more of those trophies every year since.

I am sharing this information with you here and now for two reasons:

1. Since the moment that Sam handed me those two trophies, I have been under siege by people asking me to share the hacks, habits and skills that I employ to close over $10,000,000 in sales every

year. I have spent hundreds of hours doing that at conferences, podcasts and sales summits both in person and online.

2. I have had great coaches come into my life like Sam Taggart, Coach Micheal Burt and Lightspeed VT's CEO Brad Lea. They have convinced me that I could write this very book and produce a world-class training academy titled MOD Sales Academy while in stride and not slowing down one bit from doing what I love. I am writing this preface in the winter of 2022 and finished 2021 with personal sales volume of well over 2 MW of solar sold. More importantly, the company that I help lead has signed over 20 MW in solar contracts (approximately $80,000,000 in sales) and is on its way to becoming a legendary sales organization. SunSolar Solutions had six people on stage to receive a Golden Door Award this year which was more than 25% of the recipients in the entire industry. It is with Sam, Coach Burt's, and Brad's help, expertise, and technology that I was able to write this book and launch its companion virtual training portal, MOD Sales Academy, while continuing to knock doors and close sales face to face at the very highest level.

To be perfectly honest, my true motive—other than to answer the overwhelming number of requests to offer this knowledge and training in a manner that will enable me to keep selling—is to inspire good salespeople to embark on a journey to become truly great and perhaps find their way to my company, SunSolar Solutions, or one of the many good companies leading this green-energy revolution. I want those salespeople to join a truly great company, one that is installing a technology that offers to help solve Earth's most urgent problem while transforming families' finances, wellbeing, and security. I want this book to show them how to make a seven-figure income doing it.

The Covid-19 pandemic has mostly passed, and we're at the dawn of a Green New Deal. This is the very beginning of a new era. People always ask me what I say to get people to get them to buy today. I'll cover that in depth in this book, but let me give you the short and sweet answer:

If you're not in three or four homes a day, you're not going to sell 2 to 3 million watts of solar in a year (or its equivalent in your industry).

You have to put yourself in a position to close three or four times a day. That's what I do every single day. People ask, "How do you structure your day?" I just keep working until I know I have three or four appointments tomorrow. If I don't, I know I'm not done working.

So how do you design and execute the behavior that makes this happen? You have to create what I call "No Matter Watt" habits. This is a sacred commitment to do a handful of the most doable tasks you can imagine every single day, "No Matter Watt...even if your ass falls off." Once you formulate this very simple list of tasks, you must create or join a support system that you will connect with every day and that will hold you accountable and pick you up when you inevitably fall down. If you combine the hacks, habits, and skills taught in this book with that system of accountability and support, you will find yourself able to get to those three or four kitchen or conference-room tables every day and then, once you're there, close most of them—today!

Simple, right? It can be.

You can win the equivalent of a Double Golden Door award this year. Get that idea in your head. This book is a recipe for making a multiple or high six-figure income. Perhaps you are one of the rare breeds that can use these hacks, habits, and skills to make more than $1,000,000 income annually in sales. If you follow the directions in this book and the companion MOD Sales Academy (www.MODSalesAcademyVT.com), which is not only a virtual one-on-one-sales interactive training experience but a community that can provide that support and accountability, it will become a reality. The only variable is your willingness to make a sacred commitment to doing a small number of absolutely doable actions *every day*—No Matter Watt!

I am the vice president of sales and marketing at SunSolar Solutions, and I started selling solar in 1984. Since then, I've mastered the art of setting appointments door to door and have utilized presentation and closing techniques that have resulted in over 12 million watts of solar personally sold since 2015. That's approximately $10 million in sales every year. In addition, along with my partners Troy Dinbokowitz and Val Berechet, I lead a sales team that has sold over 8,000 solar systems. That adds up to over 80 million watts of solar installed and approximately one third of a billion dollars in sales.

I want to make clear that the hacks, habits, and skills that we are going to cover in detail in this book are not my theories on sales or what I learned years ago when I used to be in sales. My job is to be at three or four kitchen tables every day six or seven days a week selling solar and closing a majority of them. I do that while meeting the responsibilities of being a principal owner of a large solar company and leading a sales force that will sign and close approximately 2,000 solar contracts valued at $100,000,000 in 2022.

Being the number-one salesperson in the industry, in addition to providing a multi-million dollar income, has led to numerous opportunities to share how I do that both one-on-one and to many people at a time at conferences and on podcasts. At first I found myself wondering why in the hell I was taking so much of my time showing a multitude of salespeople that don't work for my company how to sell much more effectively when I could be selling myself. Then I started receiving emails, texts, and DMs from young salespeople effusively expressing their gratitude for how much better they and their families were doing since they found the bits and pieces of mental strategy I teach, which derive from my own experience and from the wisdom of the immortal greats of sales, such as Napoleon Hill and Og Mandino.

My wife Marcia and I were in Key West, Florida, for a solar conference put on by my friend Bill Murphy. He had asked me to travel 3,000 miles to talk to his tribe of salespeople that belong to his very successful Solar Cheat Code. As I was in the kitchen of this mansion situated on its own island going over my outline of what I was going to share (and what I was going to hold back from this room of competitors), a young man came up to me and introduced himself. He told me that he had been able to access some videos that Sam Taggert had posted to his D2D University, which he shot with me after showing up at my house one afternoon with no warning.. The 20-something salesman told me about his first year in solar sales and how he had sold 10 or 12 systems, which was enough to keep his wife and baby afloat but not much more. He talked about listening to the videos Sam and I made almost every day. This completely knocked me out. Then he told me that for the past several months since finding my training, he had been selling 15 to 20 systems a month. He was in disbelief that he was making more money in a month than he had ever made in a year. I was so moved by my conversation with him that I couldn't begin to focus on my notes again. I left them behind and walked onto that stage and forgot everything about what I was going to hold back. Bill came onto the stage 90 minutes into my 50-minute talk to "help me" wrap it up, and he got yelled off of the stage by an audience that was not shy about wanting me to stay in the pocket, which I did for at least another hour.

That was the last time I questioned whether or not I was doing the right thing by showing up and teaching salespeople how to be successful at this noble craft. I have been more than worried that my partners Val and Troy would confront me about aiding and abetting the competition. They have been more than understanding and unquestioningly supportive. Solar has afforded us with financial success beyond anything we had ever imagined when we began this journey. We believe that it is meant to be that way because we are promoting a solution to an existential threat to the world we live in. We have been blessed with the opportunity to do well by doing good.

If having the skills to help families commit to what is often a scary investment has enabled our company to grow from 12 employees a year ago to over 150 employees today, then perhaps it is important to do what my friend Brad Lea so often says: "We have to get the knowledge from the people who have it to the people who need it."

At 57, I often get called "that old guy" who sells more solar than any of the young guys. The first chapter coming up tells the story of how I came upon one group of "old guys" who showed me how to avoid a life of cataclysmic disaster, one that was guaranteed to result in jails, institutions, and an early death. It also tells of another set of "old guys" who showed me how to get invited to the kitchen where the members of a family make their important decisions and, once there, how to give them the courage to do just that—*today*.

Can this "old guy" pass that on to you? That's why we're here. Let's go.

Part 1

The Journey to a 7-Figure Income in Sales

Chapter 1
Birth of a Salesman

When I was 10, my family moved from New York to Arizona, where I met a new crew of buddies. We used to run around back alleys, thinking we were kings. One day, we came upon several cases of what we determined to be some kind of miracle cleaner, and I had the idea to go door to door selling it.

When we first found this stuff, it didn't occur to me not to go knock on a door. My first instinct was to sell it. And it could have led to lots

25

of success, but we had a very limited inventory. When we sold it all, we didn't know how to get more. That was the end of that enterprise.

Prior to that, I was the kid that would knock on doors to sell raffle tickets to raise money for my Pop Warner football team. I would leave my house at 10 o'clock in the morning on a Saturday and not come home until I had sold every last $1 ticket. Everyone else sold three raffle tickets to their mom, dad, and uncle, and I would blow them all away. That gave me a little idea that I was pretty good at this.

So when the "miracle cleaner" came our way, I was the one in our crew on a doorstep, talking to people like I was starring in my own infomercial, expounding on the miraculous properties of this stuff. I don't even know if it was cleaner, but I just started selling the heck out of it.

When I was 12 years old, I had a paper route, and I was an awful paperboy. My paper-route manager hated me because I couldn't get up in time. But we were also supposed to sell newspaper subscriptions, and I could sell five in a night, no problem. So that saved me from getting fired.

I found selling to be invigorating, exciting. And, truthfully, my family needed the money. I started to knock on doors and sell lawn mowing jobs. Again, I was terrible at actually mowing lawns, but that didn't matter. The other guys would mow, and I would get the jobs.

At 15 years old, I got my first real job at the local pizzeria. I didn't ask how much it paid. All I knew was that people with jobs had money. I wanted money, so I knew I needed a job. Well, I worked for a month, and as it turned out, they held the first check as a deposit on the uniform. Once I finally got my first check two weeks later, it was for $87. I was confused because it didn't seem like a lot of money. My boss explained that it was $2.35 an hour plus tips. I didn't get tips, though, aside from maybe 50 cents here and there as I wiped off a table I was cleaning because it wasn't a full-service place. I'm putting in all this work, making pizzas and washing dishes, with $87 to show for it after a month. I needed a new plan.

My mom had a job one summer making calls for the Disabled American Veterans to see if people would put out clothing and household items as donations for their thrift store. It was one of several sales type jobs she did from home to help my dad who was a police officer provide for eight kids. Listening to her do that made me want to try it. I begged her to let me and after some brief supervision, she could tell I was pretty good at it and turned it over to me. She paid me $.50 for every yes. When I learned later that she got paid $2.00 for every yes, I got my first lesson on how businesses make a profit.

The idea stuck with me that you could just pick up a phone and start making money. So I turned in my apron and found a telemarketing job in the paper. A company hired me for $5 an hour selling tickets to the Policeman's Ball. I was getting paid literally twice as much per hour as I used to make, plus commission. I found I could make four or five sales (which was enough to make my boss happy) in about an hour and a half and I would spend the rest of my 2 1/2 hour shifts talking to girls on the telephone. That was the beginning of relying on my talent to hit minimums instead of pushing through to my potential. Also, I figured out very quickly that working a few hours after school for several times the money was a hell of a lot better than working nights and weekends for pocket change.

I graduated high school and went to college at the University of Pacific to get into the computer-engineering curriculum. I was on a scholarship, but I had no money. So I did what I knew best and got a job in a phone room setting appointments for a solar company. In the eighties, right after the energy crisis of the seventies, Jimmy Carter came up with the idea of offering tax credits for people who install renewable-energy devices on their homes. At the time, there was no photovoltaic solar or any other kind of solar electricity, so solar meant you had a water heater on your roof that the sun heats up. So I went to work setting appointments for salesmen selling solar water heaters. I did well enough to get promoted to supervisor, which is the person who then confirms the appointments.

One day, I saw the vice president of sales putting on a training class on how to sell solar. Now, I'm 19 at the time, but I look 14. Curious, I slipped into the back of the room and watched him show the salesmen the presentation and how to walk the customer through it in a three ring binder. I had the same thought I had watching my mother make those thrift store pick up calls: I know I can do this.

At the end, I got one of the three-ring binders, went into the phone room, and grabbed an appointment. I went out to the appointment, brought the three-ring binder, and made my first sale. I called the phone room to let them know, and the appointment setter I talked to asked if I wanted another one. I tell them yes—and I make that sale. They ask if I want another—boom, another sale.

I'm elated. I've been on three of these appointments and sold all three. I get home that night, and my phone rings. It's the vice president of sales.

He asks, "Who are you again?"

I explained that I was the kid from the phone room that was in the back of the room earlier that day. He was confused, only remembering "a young kid." I told him that that was me but that I was 19 and was the supervisor in the phone room. He said that after the day I had, I wasn't going to be in the phone room anymore—I was now a salesman. I didn't want to make the same mistake as before with the pizza parlor, so I asked how much it paid.

"Five-hundred dollars," he said.

"Wow!" I said. "I made $500 tonight!"

"Oh, no," he said. My heart sank. I knew it was too good to be true.

"These pay $500 each," he continued. "You made $1,500 tonight. Good job."

This changed my world. Not only could I do something I loved, but I could get paid well for it.

The man I met in that conference room that day was the leader of a group of "old guys" that this 19-year-old was invited to join. I was taught how to sell solar by Tin Men, who had sold aluminum siding for 30 years.

Most salespeople have seen the movie *Glengarry Glen Ross* or at least have seen the memes of Alec Baldwin telling Jack Lemmon to put down that coffee because coffee is for closers. (Remind me someday to let you in on the inside joke of the second prize for the contest being a set of steak knives). A lesser-known movie, but one that really takes you out into the field where salesmen ply their trade, is *Tin Men*. It's about the aluminum-siding salesmen of the 1960s, who used the tricks of the trade to make money for new Cadillacs and flashy lifestyles.

These old guys I was working with were some of the actual "tin men," and they had discovered solar in the 1980s and were making money selling it. They knew how to get themselves to knock on doors and use all kinds of antics to get invited to the kitchen table. They told me there was no such thing as a "be-back". They told me upfront that almost every customer was going to want to think about it and mull over exactly what to do, so you were doing paper work 15 minutes later almost every time.

I've now been a professional salesman for over 40 years. When people ask me what I sell, I always tell them the same thing: I sell whatever's moving. I was selling those first solar systems in California when I was in college in 1983. Then I spent 25 years selling in the computer industry until I noticed these complete solar systems cropping up on roofs in 2013.

In 2015, my curiosity got the better of me. I wanted to sell solar, but I was scared to death because I had golden handcuffs on. Golden handcuffs are what you have when you're working for a company and you're making good money. You know you could make more money somewhere else doing something else, but you know this business, and it pays your bills. So I moonlighted with these guys who I had been introduced to who had just started a solar company. I went out and knocked on some doors with my now partner Troy and watched him make a few presentations. I went home and got a three ring binder. I built a compelling solar presentation just like the ones the Tin Men had shown me and employed the tactics I had learned to light the prospects' ass on fire and get them signed up on the first call. I sold my first three solo presentations and seven or eight more over the next two weeks. I did the math and realized I had made more money during that period than I would have in a quarter at my corporate America salary plus bonus job. I turned in the keys to my company car and made the leap.

Over the next year, I came close to selling a million watts of solar. My breakout year came in 2017. A lot of my success that year had to do with circumstances arising from the end of net metering, which created a big deadline for Arizona homeowners. I worked like a madman through that deadline. Through the end of that year, I sold over two and a half million watts—an accomplishment no one had ever conceived of up until that time.

Chapter 2
First Things First: Kill What's Killing You

I started drinking when I was 15 and was done by the time I was 19. It's not a long story, but it's a big story. I was arrested three times and went to a grown-up jail once. I have not had a drink or a mind-alternating chemical since January 1, 1984, the day I went to my first 12 step meeting for people with substance-abuse issues. I've been clean and sober now for over 38 years, which is pretty much the entirety of my adult life.

Coach Micheal Burt talks about how closing is the act of killing something off. It's why I want you to kill what's killing you. You can do all the professional and personal development you want, but if you are in the grip of an addiction or an obsession with some sort of destructive behavior, nothing you do is going to be successful until you address that problem. Many of us are dealing with an issue that is keeping us from being successful. For me, that was alcohol and drugs. For you, it could be food, sex, gambling, obsessive-compulsive behaviour, an unhealthy relationship, or a mental illness that needs treatment or medication.. You can't start going down the positive path until you get off the negative path. Og Mandino tells us in *The Greatest Salesman in the World* that only a good habit can replace a bad habit.

I was doomed to be an alcoholic/addict centuries before I was born. I am sure there are male members of my family who are not alcoholics, but let's just say the odds of not being a member of the CIA (Catholic, Irish, alcoholic) are not very good.

A neighbor helped my mom discover what the likely problem with our constantly distressed family was. She joined a 12-step program for spouses of alcoholics and dragged all seven of my brothers and sisters to the corresponding 12-step program for children of alcoholics. At these meetings, speakers told their "story" about what had happened and what life was like now that they were in recovery from a seemingly hopeless state of mind and body.

Hearing alcoholics describe a hole in their gut that the wind blew through rang a bell for me, and that bell could not be unrung. I heard how they experienced a self-consciousness that left them debilitated in social situations. How they were constantly comparing other people's outsides with their insides and coming up woefully short. How they experienced the trauma of growing up in a family where something was terribly wrong but they were not sure what it was. I also learned that the problem resulted from a disease that could not be cured and that, once it was self-diagnosed, there was no escaping it. I learned that the fortunate ones hit a bottom that enabled them to see clearly that they were powerless to overcome the cataclysmic consequences for themselves and their family—which included personal and family ruin, jails, institutions, and death—without the aid of a power greater than themselves and a fellowship of others going through exactly the same thing.

As a sophomore in high school, I found myself at a "party," trespassing late one night on the golf course across the street from the local pizza place and holding a can of beer, scared to death to drink it. I knew the minute I did, I would find out if I was an alcoholic. I felt like I was holding a bomb. I actually poured that beer out while pretending to drink it. I did that a few more times in an attempt to avoid lighting that fuse.

My brother Joe has never had a drink in his entire life and has successfully avoided alcoholism through that strategy. Things changed one night when I was 15. I was on a double date with a girl I was very interested in and very shy around, and my buddy with the truck stopped at a convenience store and found a guy to buy us beer. I had no idea that was going to happen, but I didn't want to be the guy not in on the fun.

I drank that beer and several more as well, and we made our way to the parking lot of the pizza place where "everyone" hung out on Friday nights after football games. There was that crowd that I had always wanted to "be cool" with but never had been because my torturous self-consciousness had always made me freeze up and become quiet and standoffish. But this time, that hole in my gut was gone. I was excited to be there, and I felt like someone who should be at the center of the crowd with that very pretty girl on my arm. When I jumped out of the truck, I grabbed her by the hand, and I didn't just walk across the lot—I glided. As I approached the perimeter of that group, I didn't freeze up. I crashed through with a smile on my face and a joke on my lips. I had a pat on the back and a laugh for everyone. I was being the person I always wanted to be, and it felt great! I had such a good time. Later in the evening, the girl and I ventured onto the golf course across the street, and I rounded a base or two.

Along with the light side of being intoxicated came the dark side. I drank more beers that night and ended up being sick, which was embarrassing. While walking home late that night by myself, I inexplicably went into some random person's yard and vandalized the cute plaster-of-Paris scene that they had decorated their yard with. I ruined something that was dear to someone and took a perverse pleasure doing it.

As I walked to school Monday morning, I passed by that yard and saw the crime I had committed, and for the life of me I could not understand why I would have done that. When I got to school, I approached the cool crowd hanging out before school in the quad. I was excited to see them and was looking forward to enjoying my new personality. But as I approached, I froze. The lubrication needed for that gear was gone. I desperately tried to summon it, but to no avail. I had two depressing thoughts: first, the personal transformation that had taken place the previous Friday night was not there without alcohol, which was exactly what I had heard those alcoholic speakers talk about; second, I wanted to be that person and feel those feelings regardless of what the consequences might be. Something I had my first glimpse of, but did not fully understand until many more consequences came my way, was that when I drank I could not predict or control my behavior. I went from honor-roll student to instant criminal.

My grandmother's first cousin was "Mad Dog" Vincent Coll, who was portrayed by Nicolas Cage in the 1984 movie *The Cotton Club*. He was a notorious gangster during Prohibition and was a member of Dutch Schultz's gang. He is mostly known for trying to assassinate Schultz to take over his criminal empire in New York City. He ended up getting himself killed when his failed attempt led to Dutch Shultz's hit men riddling his body with bullets from a Tommy gun as he used a pay phone in a local bar. He wasn't much older than I was when I was arrested for selling cocaine to an undercover cop at a Talking Heads concert at UC Davis in Santa Cruz, California, right about the time the movie *The Cotton Club* debuted.

I was determined to learn the cocaine business much like Johnny Depp does in the movie *Blow*, but I was lucky enough to get myself arrested in the first five minutes of my own version of the movie. I say "lucky" because with my "instant criminal, just add alcohol" tendencies and my entrepreneurial drive, I believe I was destined to go out in a ball of flames or a long prison sentence like the guys in that movie. Instead, that blessed intervention landed me in jail for three days, where I evaluated my choices. I decided to go straight and dedicate myself to my studies at the University of Pacific, where I was studying computer engineering. I mustered all the determination and willpower I had and walked out of that jail three days later completely committed to staying clean, at least until the heat died down. It took me three hours to get back to my dorm room and four hours to find myself in front of a scale, weighing out ounces of coke and doing lines to take the edge off. That was my best shot. I took my finals high and failed most of them.

My mom sent me $125 to take a plane home for Christmas break. Instead of buying an airplane ticket, I spent $75 on a bag of really bad homegrown weed and the other $50 on a 25-hour Greyhound bus ticket. Because my behavior was so dangerously unpredictable when I drank and because I did not want to end up an alcoholic like my dad, his dad, and most of my uncles, I tended to gravitate to drugs instead of alcohol. I also envisioned drugs as more glamorous. I liked being the guy everyone was waiting for to arrive at the party. Well, sitting on a bus for 25 hours, going into the small onboard bathroom to smoke really crappy grass every half hour while getting increasingly paranoid out of my mind that the driver would pull over and serve me up to the California Highway Patrol, is not an experience anyone would call glamorous.

When I arrived in Phoenix, I was met by a friend from my teen group who listened to my entire story of woe. I was in serious trouble, and I now realized that I did not possess the power to stop on my own. At this lowest of low points, she asked me if I was willing to go to a 12-step meeting for people who have alcohol and drug problems. As bad as things were, that was the last thing on my mind. But I was open to anything that offered the promise of relief, so I said yes.

It was at the ripe old age of 19 that I met the other bunch of "old guys" in those meetings who would enable me to change my life. I was desperate to find a way to stop the spiral I was helpless to stop by myself. I was also hoping the judge would believe that I was going to meetings and had gone straight. Those old guys in those meetings told me a lot of things, including that they had spilled more on their tie than I had ever drunk. I told them they were absolutely right and that if they had not spilled so much and had tried cocaine, they would have gotten there a hell of a lot sooner.

They also told me that they had discovered the secret to successfully overcoming one of the most persistent maladies in the history of mankind. And it was so simple, they said, that they had rarely seen anyone fail who had thoroughly followed their path. Now, they did not say that it was easy. In fact, the odds of someone reaching those meetings alive and unincarcerated were not good. The odds of someone following through on the one simple requirement were not great either. They said the solution was simple—not easy. "Go to 90 meetings in 90 days," they told me. That was it. A sacred commitment to doing *one* extremely simple thing every day. So simple that even the weakest and feeblest couldn't claim not to be able to do it. Go to one meeting every day. And by "every day," they meant every day *no matter what!* Even if your ass falls off. If your ass falls off, pick it up and bring it to a meeting.

Oh, and there was a catch: don't take the first drink between meetings. In those instructions was the secret to succeeding at almost anything. The power of taking action to travel the distance between zero and one. Or the power of not crossing the line between zero and one. One drink is too many, and a thousand is never enough for an alcoholic. Willpower does not work. Motivation does not last. As we listen to some of the greatest motivational speakers of our time, we receive nuggets that fill us with a great desire to accomplish truly legendary things. Know this: motivation does not last and in the end does not work—unless you use it to forge a sacred commitment to take one simple action every day *no matter what!** (*even if your ass falls off!*)

By the way, after going to one meeting every day and not taking the first drink for six months, I finally ended up in front of that judge. I told him I'd been going to meetings, hadn't had a drink or a drug, had letters from sponsors, and didn't need to go to jail. He said that he was really glad that I was clean and sober and had the support of meetings and sponsors. But, he said, I was also going to jail.

When I asked those old guys how long I had to go to these meetings every day, they said that was simple too. You *have* to come until you *want* to come. By that time, I had come to know these guys who had sobriety and a higher power, and I wanted what they had. I also wanted to go to meetings every day. But no one could have done for me what those 45 days in jail did for me: bring me face to face with the stakes involved in the proverbial "jails, institutions, and death." I had started going to those meetings with a burning desire not to have to go to jail, but I got out of jail having forged a sacred commitment to going to one meeting every day and not taking the first drink or drug every day. That was over 38 years ago.

During my corporate America sales career I kept this part of my life to myself. If you knew me well and for any period of time, you would've figured out that I don't drink. If you would've asked me, I would've told you the story but for the most part I kept this part of my life hidden. I did much the same as I entered my solar career, but had numerous opportunities to share the story and this part of my life. The reactions to this were astounding and it was clear that I could make a difference in people's lives by sharing this openly.

Today, I talk about it on social media and from the stages I speak on. I have connected with a great number of people on a very deep level. Some of them have found themselves changing course and leaving destructive behaviors behind. There are dozens of 12 step programs that deal with every imaginable obsession and malady. If you are in the grip of one of them, I encourage and support you to reach out to one of these and/or seek professional help. I have done both and cannot imagine where I would be today without having availed myself to those resources.

Chapter 3
Solar to the Rescue

When I met Sam Taggart, the CEO of D2DCon and D2D Experts, for the first time, I was on stage with him, and he was handing me two Golden Door Award trophies. You get a Golden Door Award in solar sales at D2DCon if you have sold over a million watts of solar a year or made 100 sales. So Sam made a request for anyone who had sold over a million watts of solar to come up to the stage.

I went up and talked to the person making the list. He asked, "What did you sell?"

I told him 2.6 megawatts.

He said, "No, not the whole company. You personally."

I said, "Well, I sold and closed 2.6 million watts of solar personally, and the company that I am one of three partners of, SunSolar Solutions, sold several times that amount."

Sam wasn't quite prepared for that, and only had one-megawatt trophies. So when I came up to the stage that night, he handed me two trophies. It was done somewhat in jest, but it was certainly real. And that is how the Double Golden Door Award became a thing.

The rest of the night, everyone asked me, "How in the world did you sell more than two and a half times that amount?"

I humbly explained that part of it was Arizona's net-metering deadline. The state made a fundamental change to how electric-utility customers were going to get credit for all their surplus power, the energy they produced with their solar system but did not need at over a given period, and sold to the grid. They had declared that net metering was no longer going to be available after July 1, 2017, and that all customers who signed up before that date would be grandfathered in for 20 years; otherwise, you were out and couldn't get in. You would get the new plan which didn't yet exist and was sure to be nowhere near as good. The payment formula is a crucial element in solar accounting and a key determinant of profitability.

Before that I was doing fine, but something in me switched. I woke up to the fact that I was dealing with a countdown clock. In sales, we talk about generating urgency with the customer. The very limited amount of time that we had to sell solar with net metering had the effect of generating urgency in me, and I was then effectively communicating that urgency to the customer. The customer and I had an opportunity to take advantage of an offer that was here today and gone tomorrow. This offer was going away, and the conversation was going to be entirely different after that July 1 date. I started to understand that every hour of the day was a perishable commodity and that it was a once-in-a-lifetime opportunity that I would use or lose.

What happened next is that I started to respond in a manner appropriate to the situation. Imagine that a friend invited you to their community center over Easter weekend for an Easter-egg hunt. You join your friend as people gather for the event. You look out over the field and see all the plastic Easter eggs on the ground, up in trees, on playground equipment, and you think *this will be amusing.*

The gun goes off, and you make your way onto the field and pick up your first plastic Easter egg. There is a jelly bean inside. You think, *that's nice*, and you pick up another, which turns out to be a chocolate egg. You bend down to get your third egg, and you look inside to find $3,000. You think, *What the heck just happened? Is this a mistake? Did I just stumble onto the grand prize? Did I just get insanely lucky?* You bend down and pick up another egg, and there is a jelly bean inside. You pick up another, and there is a chocolate candy inside. You pick up one more, and there is another $3,000 inside.

Now you think that something really extraordinary is happening. You look around, and you notice that everyone on the field has the same look on their face and is looking around as well. It hits you: every third egg on this field has $3,000 in it! Let me ask you a question. Would you be thinking at this point that it was a good time to take a break, maybe leave and go to Starbucks? No, you wouldn't. You would begin to act like someone whose ass was on fire. How you imagine yourself acting at that point is exactly how I started to respond to that net-metering deadline.

I started setting appointments at 7 in the morning all the way to 10 at night. I started hitting every door with the story that they were about to miss out and get screwed over and this was their only chance to get in on this life-changing opportunity!

I went from having three or four appointments a week to four or five appointments a day—and I was closing almost every one of them. The vast majority of solar appointments end the same way. The customer is completely convinced that they need to go solar; that it is a superior financial strategy that will improve their family's net worth by a six-figure dollar amount; that they will feel terrific about being part of the solution instead of part of the problem with respect to climate change; that they will give themselves peace of mind by heading off the inflation that would double or triple their energy costs in the next 10 to 15 years; and that renting their power equipment, giving the electric company up to

$50,000 in the next ten years while getting nothing in return, is flat-out stupid; and that they would like to get the paperwork signed and the project underway...tomorrow.] Yes, after all that, they would ask, "Can you come back Friday?"

I had been closing a good percentage of my presentations on the same day by using the "today only" closed that those old aluminum-siding salesmen had taught me back in the early 1980s, but the urgency that this deadline brought to the kitchen table took things to a whole new level. It was as if there was a gun being held to the customer's head and I wasn't the one holding the gun.

I would literally tell them, "I am not coming back. I am not being rude; this is not some sales-guy tactic. I want your business, and perhaps I can come back after the deadline, but I will not have any time before. I will be in four or five of these meetings every day. We need to get this written up today if we are going to get this done on this side of the deadline. If it were up to me, there would be no deadline. This would be available forever. Let's just get this written up, and you can use the three days the state always gives you to talk to your accountant, realtor, God, whoever. Doesn't that sound like a reasonable plan?"

I learned something invaluable: that selling when the customer has a gun to their head, especially when you are not the one holding the gun, is very effective.

This was a powerful gift. Winning two Golden Door Awards in one year was a breakout accomplishment made possible by this once-in-a-lifetime circumstance that I had nothing to do with...or was it? I started to ask myself: was it possible to learn lessons from this experience and use those lessons to do this again?

This book is about the answers that came from asking questions like those. Those answers have enabled me to sell between two and three megawatts of solar every year since, earning the Double Golden Door Award in 2017, 2018, 2019, 2020, and 2021. This book isn't about theories I have or tactics I used to employ back in the days when I made a name for myself working in the field. I am still at three or four kitchen tables every single day, seven days a week, utilizing my habits, hacks, and skills of 9-figure sales that produces a 7-figure income everyday to sell millions of watts of solar right now. It's about going from being reasonably successful in sales, as I was for over 25 years, to having legendary sales results.

The "today only" close wasn't a trick. The customer literally had a limited amount of time to take advantage of the offer. So what was next? I looked for another net-metering deadline. As it turned out, Tucson was due to eliminate net metering in the next few months. My wife and I had just purchased a new home in Peoria, and I told her that we were moving to Tucson and would be renting a house there for the next few months. It turned out that the net-metering deadline was moved several times and lasted for most of the following year. We had exactly the same results, and I closed out the year having sold 2.86 MW of solar. I arrived in Salt Lake City at D2DCon to receive another Double Golden Door Award.

Something more important also happened during the course of that year. It became clear to me that the difference in my results was primarily in my mind. I was the one who was perceiving the urgency. I was the one communicating the circumstances to the customer effectively. It also occurred to me that in order to achieve this level of success, I would need to find a way to keep myself working in this gear. We're going to talk later about the nine-figure mindset and how to get your mind to perceive a worthwhile goal, such as generational wealth. We'll talk about how to get your brain and good habits to be running the show instead of bad habits and your emotions. This will propel you and your results into a new dimension.

After leaving Salt Lake City with my second Double Golden Door Award, I was on a mission to figure out how to bring this kind of urgency to every sale in every year. I was determined to figure out how to continue operating at that high level.

As it turned out, there was always something changing about the solar offer. It was my job as the expert to understand what that was and communicate it. The new credit system in Arizona went from net metering to net billing. The utilities have been very effective at negotiating a deal whereby the very high cash price being offered to the consumer in the first year after net metering would drop by 10 percent every year after that. No other solar companies were perceiving that as anything but a negative. Based on our experience and how effective the net-metering deadline was, we turned the beginning of every single year into another deadline. We also did some research on the tax credits, which are another significant component of making a solar-system investment pencil out as a profit for the customer. Well, the tax credit that had been extended in 2016 was set to fall from 30 percent to 26 percent in 2019 and then to 22 percent in 2020. Every solar company on the planet perceived this as a negative. I intuitively knew that this was a huge benefit on the sales side. If we could learn to understand the differences in the utility and the tax-credit offers and become effective at communicating those to the customer, we could bring urgency to every single solar presentation throughout each of the coming years. That's exactly what we did, and it worked perfectly.

When it comes to selling solar, it's imperative that you understand exactly what the utility and tax-credit policies are that affect the customer, as well as any other changes happening in the community. Many utilities across the country are going to be transitioning away from net metering. You need to follow what the utility-regulation boards are doing and what's being argued in front of them and then bring those arguments in front of the customer. For instance, in the Arizona market the utilities have hired consultants, who have done studies that have convinced the state utility-regulation board that the grid was designed for centralized distribution and not for distributed generation, which is what solar power-er is. These studies argue that many markets like Hawaii and California are now experiencing problems because there are too many solar systems served by individual electric substations and that there needs to be a limit. That limit has been set in the state of Arizona to 15 percent of an area served by a substation. That means that once 15 percent of the homes in an individual neighborhood install solar systems, no one else can be approved to go solar and attach their system to the grid. This effectively creates a 15-percent lid on how many homes can be solar-powered, and each and every homeowner risks being left out of solar altogether if they don't act now! Find out exactly how the utilities in your market are crediting their customers for transfer of their surplus solar production to the grid. Look for any other changes coming down the road that will cause the solar offer to change significantly.

Solar was granted a gift from heaven in January of 2021. The tax credits were due to drop from 26 percent to 22 percent on January 1 and then disappear altogether at the end of this year. January 1, 2022, was going to mark the first day with zero federal tax credits for consumers to go solar. As part of the Covid-19 relief bill passed in January of 2020, those tax credits were extended at the 26-percent level for an additional two years, at which time they are set to fall and go away again. How perfect! For several years we've had the opportunity to pitch solar with the crucial fact being that the tax credits were going away, and then, at the 11th hour and 59th minute, they were extended for two more years, at which time they would be going away again! Once again, the customer has a gun pointed to their head, and they must move forward with going solar or else go solar without tax credits. Why will they be going solar without tax credits? That same Covid-19 relief bill that extended the tax credit was the first part of the current administration's plan to get rid of fossil fuels altogether in the next 10 to 15 years. The extension of the tax credit is the carrot. What follows is the stick. The new administration has re-entered the Paris Climate Accord, which essentially volunteers the

United States to impose carbon taxes on itself and thereby increase the cost of fossil fuels. This will accelerate the growing cost of kilowatt-hours to a blinding rate. Welcome to America's Green New Deal!

Typically, the cost of kilowatt-hours has doubled every 15 years for the last 60 years. That was before the current administration's moon-shot: its commitment to end the use of fossil fuels in the next 10 or 15 years. This will have the same effect on coal-generated electricity as the government's anti-tobacco measures had on cigarette prices. Initially we were giving warnings that cigarette smoking was killing everyone. The warnings were put on the labels. Nobody quit smoking cigarettes. I grew up in the '60s and '70s, and my parents smoked three packs of cigarettes a day. My mom would be driving and smoking with one hand and trying to smack kids that weren't wearing seatbelts with the other. No one was paying any attention to the warning labels. It wasn't until cigarettes went from 60 cents per pack to over $8 per pack that people started to quit in droves...for their health, of course. Today we are being warned that the climate is changing at a dangerous pace and the polar bears will soon have nowhere to live. And what are we doing? Buying more and bigger SUVs. In the near future, fossil fuels will go from 60 cents a pack to over eight dollars a pack, and we will respond by stopping the production of internal-combustion engines and starting to care about the polar bears.

As this book is coming to print in the winter of 2022, inflation has just hit unprecedented levels of nearly 8%. The United States has banned the import of Russian oil, which has taken gasoline and energy prices at the pump to never seen before historic levels. The federal reserve has just increased interest rates for the first time in years and are telling us that this will be the first of at least six additional rate increases coming in the near future. On top of this, the Biden administration's successful infra-structure legislation has passed and will be taxing fossil fuels to pay for almost $2 trillion of future infrastructure upgrades. At the same time, the administration's Build Back Better legislation has stalled, which would have increased and extended the solar investment tax credits. This means that the stick is coming. It also looks like that the carrot will be taken away partially at the end of 2022 and the rest of it after 2023. The historic phenomenon of energy price is doubling every 15 years now looks like a pattern of the past which went along with Ronald Reagan like inflation and interest rates. In the dawn of this post-Covid era with surging interest rates and fuel prices and disappearing tax credits, there's an urgency to the need for families to go solar unlike anything we've ever seen before.

Investigate what is going on with the utility credits and policies. Understand the time-sensitive nature of the tax credits. Be able to speak intelligently about inflation and rising interest rates and the effect that will have on a family's future energy costs. Incorporate those issues into the conversation and help the customer understand that this is an urgent, dire situation. That should be your stance at the door. That should be your posture in the house. And that's what your focus should be when the customer says, "This is awesome! I'm really glad you came. Of course, we are going to need a couple of days to think about it."

After making the jump to selling solar in the first place, I was really under the gun to replace my corporate sales income. I was able to use my talent to do that quickly, which made an impression on the partners. I was offered a partnership in the company. Soon afterward, with my income surpassing my bills to the point that I was able to eliminate the $40,000 in debt that came with 25 years of "successful living," I found myself trending downwards. I was experiencing diminishing intent.

If I looked at my calendar and saw I had no appointments until 4 o'clock the next day, I found myself sleeping in till 10:30 am and lounging around until I had to jump in the shower. The problem with selling in a field where the product is moving is that you can operate at that level and still be pulling in enough cash to keep the crisis at bay. However, you cannot operate at that level and continue to be impressive. My partner

Val had a "come to Jesus" talk with me, letting me know that the reason they had made me a partner is that I showed great promise for much better results than I was delivering. I had to take a hard look at why that was.

Of course, that was after making very compelling arguments and excuses that justified my current results. But it was clear to me that the time had come to make a decision on whether the last third of my career was going to show just as much promise and deliver the same meager results as the first two thirds. I had always thought of myself as someone who would do significant things. I had already started to settle into the idea that a career with bright spots but mediocre results was something I could live with.

I made a decision. I committed not to reaching my potential but to calibrating my effort so as to deliver the results I had implicitly promised. Then I could try to hang on to and maintain my position in a company that seemed to have a lot of promise. In the course of putting in that effort, my numbers returned to being respectable, and I got into a gear just as the planets lined up for a once-in-a-lifetime opportunity.

I was repeating the same pattern that had made me an instant success but a mediocre performer over the long term in every sales job I had ever had. Inspired by a new opportunity and a new set of bosses to impress, I broke out with a flurry of effort in prospecting and cold calling. I would jump out front and get lots of attention but would quickly figure out how to make quota and get by on the connections that led from that early effort. What would my results have been in any one of those jobs if I had maintained that energy and directed it toward knocking on new doors?

Let me be clear that "knocking on doors" refers here to making cold calls: calling a prospect you have never interacted with and asking for an opportunity to present what your company has to offer. That can and does take many forms. Telephone calls, working trade-show booths, asking contacts for introductions and referrals. But many of you who are reading this will try to convince yourselves that your product or market doesn't lend itself to knocking on doors. You're wrong. Ultimately, all sales stem from the moment a salesperson asks a new prospect, one whom their company has never considered doing business with, to take a look at what they have to offer. I would venture to bet that most salespeople can trace most of their income and value to a stunningly small number of actual cold calls.

I was operating at a pretty decent level when I realized that the opportunity that I was presenting to customers was literally going to be over in a very short period of time. As you know, the net-metering deadline was what kicked me in gear to be the number-one solar salesman in the world. I was able to direct my ability and talent toward making that happen—toward somehow working at such a pace that I did not stop unless I had those four or five appointments set up for the next few days.

I had never in my life given anyone who knew me reason to be concerned that I was a workaholic. Yet I started to put in hours and work at a frenetic pace that I had never experienced before. What was a surprise to me was that my day was now filled with excitement and satisfaction instead of anxiety and dread. I quit counting commissions and started reaching for big goals. One of the conditions that made this seem possible was the existence of a definite finish line. I could rest later, I told myself; for now, I would sprint the remaining distance to the end and break the tape.

And then something absolutely unexpected and bewildering happened. On June 30, as I walked into the office with the last five contracts from the last five appointments, which had started at 8 in the morning and finished at 10 o'clock at night, my partner Val told me that it was looking as though the Corporation Commission was going to punt on the deadline. Some disagreement had arisen, and there had been a decision to consider several issues. The deadline was extended by an undetermined length of time, possibly 30 or 45 days.

I literally had tickets for my wife and me to travel to Italy, and we were going to spend an entire month and several tens of thousands of dollars touring Italy and checking off several bucket-list items. I had mixed emotions about the news that, after running a 26-mile marathon, I had an opportunity to pick myself up and immediately commence running another 26 miles. I believed that the pace at which I was going was predetermined by the fact that the motivating circumstance was only going to last so long. Now the entire picture had changed.

I knew that I could sign five solar contracts in a day, so now that the gun to the customer's head had reappeared, how could I not put it to use? I went home, slept for a day and a half, and got back on the horse. As it turned out, that deadline was moved several times. When the smoke cleared and I counted up how much solar I had sold, it was well over 2,000,000 watts of solar. Prior to that time, an absolutely spectacular year would have been 1,000,000 watts. I had somehow managed to sell twice that amount in only nine months. The income generated from that effort was literally staggering.

A funny thing happened: I didn't find myself wanting to re-book the trip to Italy and disappear for a month. I wanted to get back into an appointment the very next day and figure out what the next leg of this journey was going to look like and how we were going to close the same amount of solar on the other side of that deadline.

I wanted to be the guy I had represented myself to be. What is your why? Is it generational wealth? Is it to create a space for your family? Is it to create financial independence? I am very specific with my goals. It's in my mind, and I'm working toward it every day. I wrote down "author of a bestselling book" five years ago. I had no idea I was going to write a book. I had no intention of writing a book. Well, it's actually happening.

If you get your brain to put that into your head, then that's what's going to happen.

There is nothing that will move you further toward being able to reach your goal than the formation of habits. The only reason I'm able to have the results that I have is because of habits. It's because I have non-negotiable "no matter what" habits. You form them by getting up in the morning when you don't want to be up.

Nobody needs a habit for the stuff they like to do. I don't need to form a habit to go to the coffee pot and make coffee. You can count on me. I'm reliable when it comes to getting the coffee on in the morning. Whenever I wake up, you know I'm going to be at that coffee pot. So that's where I keep my vitamins. I have a mini-habit.

At my age, you're supposed to take an 81-milligram aspirin every day. It can be the difference between living to 60 or living to 90. But I couldn't get myself to take it. I just didn't have the ability to form habits. What I'm talking to you about is teaching yourself how to form habits—not just intellectually learning the principles of habit creation, but actually putting those principles to use and forming real habits.

The whole idea of mini-habits is momentum. Have you ever had to motivate yourself to clean the garage? A funny thing happens. It is so overwhelming at first that you would rather put a bullet in your head, but as soon as you start, you can't stop.

Momentum is a very difficult thing to break, but it's also a very difficult thing to get started. That is the idea of a No Matter Watt habit. I liken it to Newton's first law, which says that an object in motion tends to stay in motion and that an object at rest tends to stay at rest. So the whole idea of a mini-habit is to trick yourself into going from standing still, with static inertia, to being in motion, with dynamic momentum.

Chapter 4
It Matters What You Sell and Who You Sell it For

Most sales books and sales training starts with how to sell. You need to back up and realize that it truly matters what you are selling and who you are selling it for. It's imperative that you honestly believe that your product and your company are going to provide benefits and will dramatically improve your customers' lives. If you don't believe that, then mastering the techniques to sell something you don't believe in might bring you short-term success but will never bring you the lasting success you yearn for.

It matters whether you're selling a product that has demand in the marketplace. I was watching Tiger Woods win a US Open amateur championship, and after they interviewed him, they interviewed the local club champion who was paired with him.

This local golfer found a microphone in his face, and he was asked the question, "What do you do?"

He answered, "I'm in sales."

The commentator asked him, "What do you sell?"
He responded, "Whatever is moving."

That might sound like a funny response, but it has a lot of wisdom in it. If you are trying to sell a product that does not want to move, no amount of salesmanship will turn that into a tremendous opportunity. If you are not selling a product that truly helps people and has tremendous demand, then I recommend you take a hard look around and find one that does.

It matters who you're selling for. It matters that you can sleep at night and not fear the phone ringing in the morning. One of my best friends had some monumental success selling a product referred to as "biz ops." You've seen ads for companies that help you start your own business so you can work from home and make millions over the Internet. While a company and a product that truly help people start their own business and be successful could be amazing, this company was using smoke and mirrors to sell a dream to desperate people who had no money but could be talked into leveraging their last $7,000 of credit-card debt in hopes that the salesman's confidence came from the knowledge that his company would truly deliver the opportunity promised. The product had little or no cost for the company and delivered no value.

He was making tremendous money working for a guy that was the iconic leader in that space. He was tremendously successful until the FBI and US attorney general shut that company down and put that leader in jail, which led to him to committing suicide.

It matters whether the company you're working for is truly great at delivering the product or service that you are selling. I was once hired by the CEO of a company out of Austin, Texas, that had found a lucrative niche: providing outsourced technicians to do data telecommunications full-time on big campuses. They would relocate all the voice and data devices on employees' desks in an environment that saw 10 percent of its population change every month. They had created a business model whereby they could provide that service to a big company at a much lower cost than it could do for itself, and it could do it very well.

Unfortunately, the calling card for that business was selling large voice- and data-communication installation projects. My job consisted of selling those large projects and then trying to sell the service contracts afterward. The problem was that while the company was very good at the service and was extremely good at selling, they were actually terrible at delivering on those large projects in my market. They were pretty good at it in their home market in Austin, but in our branch office in Phoenix, my customers were very disappointed over and over again. I had a tremendous affection for that company and believed in the recurring-revenue model being sold to Fortune 500 companies, but every time I had a chance to prove ourselves, a customer ended up being dissatisfied.

I had been calling on a hospital system that planned on doing $10 million worth of project cabling, which would lead to a multimillion-dollar annual service contract. Every person in the organization who had input on that decision wanted to give the business to me except for the newly hired vice president of telecommunications. He wanted to pick a company that he had used in the past and was great at these projects. After much deliberation, a decision was made to split the business between the two companies. My competitor got off to a great start, and my company dropped the ball immediately. I was traveling back to New York for a big wedding when I received a call, and I was told that no sooner had we been awarded the contract than it had been completely stripped away.

I literally got on a red-eye flight and arrived at the office of the vice president of telecommunications. While in New York, I bought a fedora, which I had always wanted. When he arrived at his office at 7:30 in the morning, I was sitting in his lobby literally with my hat in my hand. He could not refuse to see me, but he would not sugarcoat his feedback.

He told me, "Michael, my job is on the line here, and I've got to place my bets with a company I have confidence will make me look good. You're an impressive sales guy, and all of my people are fighting me tooth and nail because they like you and they want to do business with you. I'll give you some advice. If I were you, I'd go work for a company that was good at what you're selling."

I was completely crestfallen and heartbroken, but I still had tremendous affection for the company I was working for and couldn't consider leaving. That evening, my telephone rang, and it was the owner of the competitor who had now been given all of the business. I considered this company to be the Darth Vader of our industry because as my competitor, I saw it as the enemy and somehow probably evil. The hospital executive had had a conversation with him that day and had offered him the inverse of the advice that he had offered me: that even though he had a terrific delivery company, he had better consider hiring a world-class salesperson if he wanted to continue to win business. That led him to calling me personally at home that night.

At first, I couldn't imagine working for Darth Vader. But then he invited me to come to his business and show me around. I couldn't resist the idea of getting to look under the hood of this Formula One race car. But I also knew that I would not be jumping ship. As he walked me around this huge building that had warehouse space, an entire department of engineers, a service department with people that appeared to be jumping to it, and a beehive of cubicles filled with people who were performing the tasks that enabled their company to deliver at such a high level, it dawned on me: how much would I be able to sell if I had a company like this delivering the product and then the services?

That tour came with an offer I could not refuse and led to me turning in my notice with a heavy heart. It also led to a four-year journey during which I immediately clicked into gear. I was suddenly able to sell eight figures of telecommunications-infrastructure projects and services per year, which catapulted my income to a level I couldn't imagine while still with the previous company. I had achieved a six-figure income there and couldn't imagine leaving, but then I opened my mind to what I could achieve if I were selling for a company that was great at what it does. That decision led to me multiplying my income several times over and over, becoming one of the top salespeople in that industry.

If you don't know in your heart—not just believe, but know—that what you are selling and who you are selling it for are going to deliver real value and provide the benefits you are promising, then stop selling it today. Go find a product and a company that will. If it makes sense, start that company yourself.

What I'm going to teach you can be used either for the benefit of, or to the detriment of, your customer. You will not be successful over any period of time if it's fake, if it's a fraud, or if it just plain sucks. There are too many good companies with good products out there to waste your time and lose your self-worth selling something that does not make your customers' lives dramatically better off.

My methods will have you handing a pen to a prospect to sign contracts for many thousands, tens of thousands, or perhaps millions of dollars, and 90 percent of the time they will be signing those documents without reading 98 percent of what's in them. They are relying on the trust and rapport that this book will help you to develop. Do not violate that trust.

Do not waste time selling for a sales-prevention team. Work for a company that is dedicated to providing the tools and processes that will make you successful. I am very fortunate to have helped start a company called SunSolar Solutions, which was built by my partner Val Berechet around two great sales people, myself and my other partner Troy Dinbokowitz, with the idea that everything that can be done to make salespeople efficient and successful should be done. We have built a Formula One race car around great talent so it can lap the competition. Don't make the mistake of going to work for a competitor that offers 50 percent more commission only to find out it's because their lack of expertise and business processes guarantee you will sell less than half as much. As the saying goes, "You get what you pay for." Or, better said, "You don't get what you don't pay for." It is true for the consumer, and it is also true for you the salesperson. If a company pays too much in commissions, they won't have the gross margin to hire the customer-service representatives, engineers, designers, and installers needed to make the company truly great.

All too often I have seen a good salesperson switch companies to make an extra 5 percent, or an extra five cents per watt in the solar industry, only to find out that selling for that company required them to basically run their own little company making sure the customer received accurate proposals and then had the product delivered properly. When you're selling and negotiating, you're always looking for a win-win. Make sure that you're working for a company that understands this, and don't seek to negotiate a compensation plan that is a win-lose. The first one to lose will be the customer, and the next one to lose will be you.

Part 2

Create Your 9-Figure Mindset

Chapter 5
The Importance of a 9-Figure Mindset

What does it mean to have a nine-figure mindset? Why should that be a goal you consider for yourself? In 1998, I cofounded an Internet company called Visitalk.com. Our first investor and the board member for all our angel investors was a young man who had made a bazillion dollars starting and selling an Internet service provider (ISP) and one of the first colocation data centers, which is known today as a cloud-computing center. When I asked him why he continued to work so hard even though he was worth tens of millions of dollars, he explained to me that the ultimate net worth is about $100 million or a low multiple of that number. That's the amount of money that a person could use to maximize their lifestyle and legacy while being anonymous and not having the publicity problems of being a billionaire. With a $100-million net worth, you can have homes on both coasts, in the mountains, in Montana, and another in the beautiful winter climate of my home in the desert, along with the private jets and helicopters to get between them all.

With good money managers, which come free with that amount of money, you should also have a passive income of more than $10,000,000 a year. This is enough to fund a lifestyle with personal helicopters and jets and the ability to do pretty much anything a person can think of. It should also give you the ability to set up a dynasty trust, which will put all your family's future generations through college. You would also have the resources to set up a foundation that makes a true and meaningful impact on the lives of needy people or on the health of the planet itself. For our investor and his partner, it has kept them in a position to be the anonymous version of Mark Cuban, running their own private shark tank and investing in the coolest technologies coming to the planet over the last 20 years. Of course this also has added greatly to their wealth.

Is this an outrageous or an outlandish goal? Not in America. Not in this day and age. I know there are hundreds, perhaps even thousands, of people who started with nothing and today have achieved this and are living that life.

How do you get there? I'm sure there are numerous paths. If I could wave a magic wand, I would invent a battery the size of a refrigerator that held gigawatts of power and cost $10,000. It would be able to transmit that power wirelessly anywhere in the world. Presto, I would've overshot my goal and would be a billionaire. I would also be in history books with Edison and Tesla.

The more common way to get there—and much more likely if, like me, you're not a genius—is to become a recognized expert in a field that is important to the planet's future and learn how to sell that product at a level that makes you extremely valuable to a company in that industry. Next, you work hard in that industry, becoming indispensable while building a personal net worth that puts you in a position to take a stake in a company. Then, build a company that is very successful at selling the product or service until someone comes along and offers to buy it for a few hundred million dollars. Presto, you have a nine-figure net worth.

When I created my chief purpose and its attendant goals, one of the items on the list was to be the author of a bestselling book. Before I wrote that down, I did not have a clear idea that that would ever happen. Now you're reading these words on this page. When I wrote down that I wanted to have a seven-figure net worth and create generational wealth, I had no clear idea of how I would navigate through life into a position where that could become real. Today I am a partner in a world-class solar company that is approaching $100 million a year in sales and will multiply that tenfold in the next few years, and someone will come along and want to buy that company for several hundred million dollars.

Incidentally, another item on that list is to have a meaningful impact on the health of this planet. As of this writing, I have sold well over 1,000 solar systems personally and help lead a company that has sold over 8,000 systems. The environmental impact in terms of carbon emissions alone from this feat is hundreds of millions of pounds saved every year. Locally, the Arizona desert we live in will not have to extract billions of gallons of water to feed the power plants that power the homes and electric cars of its inhabitants.

Why should you want to sit down right now and put your life's hopes, dreams, and visions on paper along with your chief objective and repeat those every single day out loud, as suggested by Napoleon Hill in *Think and Grow Rich*? Because if you don't, you will continue being very successful at mediocre, unimpressive goals that you are afraid to say out loud and probably don't even acknowledge. You literally have nothing to lose. Have some fun with this. Most importantly, do it now and make a sacred commitment to write those things down and read them out loud every single day. I guarantee you, not that all of those dreams will come true, but that your life will change and that the results you begin to experience will be very different from what they would have been if you hadn't done this.

Chapter 6
Create Your 9-Figure Morning

My day consists of a series of tasks, which lead to appointments, which lead to me accomplishing my goals in a way I never would've thought was possible before. My day starts at 6 am every day with a series of "No Matter Watt" habits, which I have incorporated into another morning program I have been using lately called the Miracle Morning, which is spelled out in the book by the same name by Hal Elrod. I had an opportunity to meet Hal when he spoke to our small Mastermind Circle backstage before he gave his keynote address at D2DCon one year. If you really want to take your results to a much higher level, I highly recommend this book to help you incorporate your mini-habits into the Miracle Morning.

The miracle morning is at a completely different level. It starts the night before with an affirmation of how great you are going to feel when you wake up. This counteracts the thoughts that you're not going to get enough sleep and that you're going to feel terrible in the morning. As Hal says, your last thoughts before going to sleep heavily influences your first thoughts after waking up. It begins the next morning with an alarm clock placed across the room, which begins a simple sequence called "the five-step method to break the snooze button habit." I have said for many years that I am not just a morning person—I am the worst morning person. Every single day of my life that I have set an alarm, I have hit the snooze button not once but numerous times. As it turns out, a lot of alarm clocks will stop resetting after the snooze button is hit a certain number of times, and I have found that number on many occasions. I literally had no ability to decide what time my day would start. I have not hit the snooze button one single time since I started using this very simple sequence. I highly recommend you get *Miracle Morning* today and try it out.

Every day, you set your alarm for 30 or 60 minutes before your first commitment of the day. For me, that's 5:50 in the morning. I have one hour to spend doing a sequence of tasks known by the acronym SAVERS.

Silence. five or ten minutes of silence. Just straight meditation, letting the universe speak to you instead of you speaking to the universe.

Affirmations. I caught myself saying I'm terrible at putting my seatbelt on. What you tell your brain, your brain starts to believe. So if I tell myself I'm terrible at putting my seatbelt on, I'm going to remain terrible. Now I tell myself I'm great at putting my seatbelt on, and my success ratio has gone from putting my seatbelt on 20 percent of the time to about 85 to 90 percent. You can create affirmations about anything. For me, every single morning I say the following:

- I am the number-one solar salesperson in the world.
- I am the leader of a legendary sales force.
- I am a leader of a world-class company.
- I am the author of a bestselling book.
- I am a person who will have a nine-figure net worth by 2028.

Visualizations. I see myself standing in front of big groups consulting. I see myself standing on a stage in front of my sales team, but the audience looks like the one at D2DCon and they all work for SunSolar Solutions. I see myself where I want to be. I envision it. It's not a goal, but a vision for your own life. Spend ten minutes visualizing yourself writing a check for a million-dollar home. Or taking your family on a bucket-list vacation. Those are visions.

Exercise. This is not necessarily your whole workout, but you spend 10 minutes or so exercising. It could start with one pushup that turns into 20.

Reading. I read two pages of two or three books. I recommend starting with *Mini-Habits* and then moving on to *Miracle Morning*, and then finishing up with *Think and Grow Rich*, by Napoleon Hill. This whole process falls right in line with his prescription for reprogramming your brain. You do that by reading out loud a daily mantra that describes your chief objective and all your visions and goals coming true by certain dates. I do this out loud with my wife Marcia every day.

Scribing. I have a notebook that I start each day with and list and check off my mini-habits and my SAVERS tasks. Then I use the notebook to record who is on my Cleaners' Club call every morning. Each day I find something to write about from the morning experience. That often leads to actual writing, which has led to this book.

Give yourself this hour, and this hour will reward you with a tremendous head start to your day. You will transition into your workday with a mindset and a velocity that you will hardly recognize. You will be prepared to make the most of the opportunities coming at you that you otherwise most likely wouldn't even see coming.

At 8:00 a.m seven days a week, I host a Zoom call with my top producers called the No Matter Watt Club. For several years, we called this meeting the "Cleaners' Club" as an homage to what Tim Grover calls "cleaners" in his book *Relentless*. He writes about his work with "cleaners," such as his clients Michael Jordan and Kobe Bryant. The meeting is an inspiration, accountability and support call that we started after hearing Tim Grover speak at D2DCon and turning real inspiration into a No Matter Watt habit. The call starts with a reading from an inspiration source such as Tim Grover's *Relentless* or his most recent book *Winning.* We also read from *Miracle Morning, Think and Grow Rich,* or Og Mandino's *Greatest Salesman in the World.* I attribute much of my success in my sales career to having read and followed each of the directions contained in *The Ten Scrolls From the The Greatest Salesman in the World* out loud for 30 days each. I don't think it's a coincidence that today I am the number-one salesperson in my industry.

Each of these is a textbook on things to *do* to take your sales performance to its utmost potential. Each person checks in on their No Matter Watt habits, the behavior commitments they have accomplished in the past 24 hours, and what they're committing to doing in the next 24 hours. This call started as a sacred commitment with one other person to check in every day for 90 days so that we could increase our chances of hitting an important goal. That transformed into a No Matter Watt habit itself that has led to me being on that call every day for several years. My day usually finishes up at about 10 o'clock at night after I have been in several meetings dealing with the management and ownership of Sun-Solar Solutions, done two or three presentations at kitchen tables, and knocked on at least one door and gotten one no between each of those appointments. I sometimes look back and wonder how in the world a lazy and undisciplined guy like me could have just gone through a steady 12 to 14 hours of super-productive work while not doing anything that I don't like to do.

That is really the secret. Once you have truly formed a habit, you no longer have to think about doing the work. That's the beauty of a habit. You transfer the task primarily to your subconscious mind. You do not have to remind yourself or talk yourself into brushing your teeth. If you get into bed and have not brushed your teeth or find yourself in your first meeting of the day having not brushed your teeth, you will be very uncomfortable. The difference between a task and a habit is that if you do not do the habit, you have an itch that must be scratched. You are not comfortable in your own skin. You need to get out of bed, go to the vanity, and brush your teeth—or leave the meeting and find a way to freshen your mouth.

Speaking of dental hygiene, my dentist and hygienist would lecture me to floss my teeth at every six-month visit. Don't be impressed by that regularity; it only happens because my wife Marcia insists on scheduling it no matter how annoyed I get with her for doing so. It is also because she insists on rescheduling every time I cancel due to scheduling issues. I would struggle to remember to floss and would force myself to do it, and as a result I would do it maybe a couple of times a week. One of the motivations to create a good habit is to cause a desired result. Perhaps a stronger motivation is to avoid a harsh consequence.

On my first visit to the dentist when I was six years old, I had six cavities and had to spend hours in the chair. It was only then that I became motivated to follow my mother's orders to brush every morning and every night. It was only after my wife complained about my breath that I realized it was coming from decaying meat caught in several food traps in my mouth. It occurred to me that she was not the only one noticing it and that if my job was to have people enjoy being in conversations with me, I would need to get my flossing rate to 100 percent. I created a mini-habit of getting out my floss pick before I brushed and flossed one tooth. Now who the hell can floss only one tooth? But that is precisely the idea. I am now a person who flosses every day. My wife, dentist, and hygienist are very happy about that, and so am I. A salesperson's appearance and hygiene are essential. If you're not at 100 percent on flossing let me be the one to tell you that you need to up this part of your game.

You can create a No Matter Watt habit for literally anything you want to achieve a desired result in. I have had some fun and great results following the suggestion Stephen Guise gives in *Mini Habits* to create activity cues for new habits. I can't start my coffee until I get my vitamins and put them on a plate. Marcia wanted me to help keep our glass shower enclosure sparkling clean, which requires squeegeeing the water drops off after every shower. As she is telling me to do this, she says, "I know there is no way someone with your level of ADD will actually do this, but...." So, I took that as a challenge and created a cue that before I could reach for my towel and dry off I had to grab the squeegee and do one panel. It doesn't matter how short I am on time, I cannot get out of the shower without getting the glass sparkling, and it takes less than 30 seconds.

What is a millionaire mindset? In *Think and Grow Rich*, Napoleon Hill wrote, "Whatever the mind can conceive, the mind can believe and achieve." If you can see the life you will be living after you have achieved a multimillion dollar income, invested in companies, started businesses that were sold to other businesses for hundreds of millions of dollars, and if you can believe that all that can become real, then your mind and body can get to work making it a reality. When I started this transformation, I was over 50 years old and had been working under the illusion that I had been successful for a long time. I had been successful at some unacknowledged goals to be able to pay my bills and not end up bankrupt. Oh, and maybe I will have enough when I retire to afford a respectable upper-middle-class lifestyle. I had fantasies that I would end up with a nine-figure net worth and the attendant lifestyle, but I had no illusions that I was on my way there. My search for ways to repeat the results that I stumbled upon in my first breakout year in solar led me to a set of behaviors, which have become habits, which have me on track to achieve a nine-figure net worth. I have a plan, and day by day, the pieces of the puzzle are miraculously, but not surprisingly, falling into place.

After I crashed through that first deadline and sold 2.6 million watts of solar that year, I walked over to the bank, wrote a check, and paid off my mortgage. Then my wife and I decided that maybe we should move out of the tract home with the tiny lot and the two-story house right behind us looking down at our little pool. The next year, after selling even more, I asked my brother-in-law Rob Harris to show us homes in Peoria,

Arizona, in an area that's come to be called the Upper West Side. Marcia and I were telling him that we wanted to be on this side of town and find something modest in size since our children were grown and maybe enough room to have a small office. He showed us a couple of homes that fit that description but then had the insight to show us what he believed we were actually wanting and really looking for.

We looked at a beautiful custom home on a half-acre property, measuring 3,600 square feet of floor space along with a casita. It was exactly the type of home we had always wished to be able to live in. We had always wanted to be on a half-acre of land, but it was literally double the price of what our small, fear-based thinking had in mind. We listened to Rob and looked at the life we were beginning to conceive of, and we put in the offer. Rob then came to us with the good news that our offer was accepted. "I'll have my mortgage guy call you in the morning and get the process started to get the loan approved," he said.

I said, "I don't think I'm going to need a mortgage."

He was confused. The price of the house was several times as much as our current home. "What do you mean you don't need a mortgage?"

"Marcia and I have talked about it and I think we're just going to write a check and own it outright".

Then he said, "Well, we better hurry up and get your current home sold to move your equity over."

"Actually, Rob, we've been talking about that too, and I think we're going to keep that home and rent it out."

He gave me a weird look and said, "Maybe I should quit real estate and start selling solar." Rob has a very successful real-estate business, so he didn't quit that. He and my sister Kerry, however, have become my largest source of referrals to all of their friends and clients.

That's when it occurred to me that this business I had been in for a little more than a year had really changed my life. That's when I really started to ask myself, *How am I going to create the urgency in myself to keep producing at this level?*

I knew that I did not have the answers. The truth is, I am a pretty lazy, undisciplined guy. I like to go to bed at 2 o'clock in the morning and wake up at 10:30 in the morning. As I was asking this question, I came upon a free ticket to a sales conference in Salt Lake City happening in early January called D2DCon. I have no idea where it came from. I think a vendor may have sent it without talking to me. I had not previously been someone who invested in a lot of sales training or conferences, but the ticket was free, and the idea of a bunch of guys in the door-to-door world getting together sharing tips and secrets sounded like a great idea.

I bought a plane ticket to Salt Lake City for myself and two of the people on my appointment-setting team, which included my daughter Katherine, who was my first recruit and who to this day is one of my right-hand people helping lead a door-to-door group that is one of the engines of my solar company. The first speaker was Jeremy Andrus, who had previously been one of the founders of Skullcandy and was currently the CEO of Traeger Grills. He regaled us with stories of helping to start a company that made it big and eventually was sold for big money. He also talked about using those proceeds to find a business that he could really sink his teeth into and turn into a global phenomenon. In the course of telling us that tale, he talked about the work he did to shift into the gear necessary to operate at his current level of performance. He talked about mentorship and some of the books that had really made a difference for him. He said something that stuck out to me. He talked about a book called Mini Habits by a guy named Stephen Guise. Some of the people around me seemed to have heard of that book and were aware of the idea of doing one push-up to get in shape. He acknowledged that it sounded absurd but said that the basic concept was a breakthrough that had made a world of difference for him.

I wrote down the name of that book in my notes and ordered it from Amazon on the plane ride home. It arrived a day later, and I was determined to read through the 120-page book in the next couple of hours. However, the author suggested I try something different. He recommended creating my first mini-habit by making an ironclad commitment to read two pages of this book per day and no more until it was finished.

And so I did. I read two pages of that book, which included the part about doing one push-up. I got on the floor to do one push-up and ended up doing 20 push-ups and 10 pull-ups on the bar my housemate had installed. Being an avid reader, I needed something else to read. . I told my housemate that the new book I was reading would only let me read two pages a day, so I needed something else to read. He handed me a book and asked if I had ever read *Think and Grow Rich* by Napoleon Hill. I told him that like the hundreds of self-development and sales books that I owned I had probably read a third to a half of it before I lost focus and set it aside years ago. So I picked it up and read two pages of *Think and Grow Rich*. I could not remember ever having picked up a nonfiction self-development book and reaching the final page. My new habit of reading two pages out of each of these books each day and doing my best to implement the ideas in each of them led me to completing both of them and earnestly trying to put the concepts to work.

I know what you're saying. What in the world could be accomplished by doing one push-up a day or reading two pages of a book per day? What would be accomplished if you did one push-up a day for a year? At the very least, you would have done 365 pushups and would be a lot better off for it. It is surprising to discover the cumulative benefits of accomplishing an absurdly small task once every day. John Maxwell in his books and speeches calls it the "power of one." Notice I did not say "accomplishing goals." Mini-habits are not goals. Mini habits are the checkmarks you get by going from zero to one!

Jerry Seinfeld talks about how daunting it is to have to come up with the material for an entirely new special and how that causes him to do nothing for that day. He contrasts that with looking at a calendar knowing he has to have a checkmark on every day that he wrote down at least one sentence. In the process of putting a checkmark on every single day, month after month, he is able to arrive at the goal of having an entire new hour of comedy ready for prime time.

These are behaviors that you commit to doing every day that accomplish two crucial things. First, it overcomes the first part of Newton's first law of motion, which says that an object at rest tends to stay at rest unless acted on by a force. The No Matter Watt habit is a force that takes you from the state of rest, also called static inertia, and transitions you to a state of motion in the direction of your actual goal. That enables you to take advantage of the second part of Newton's second law of motion, which says that an object in motion tends to stay in motion unless acted upon by an outside force, which now provides the benefit of momentum.

My corollary to this theorem is that a salesperson on the couch tends to still be on the couch 15 minutes from now, whereas a salesperson knocking on a door tends to be at another door 15 minutes from now. Once you transition from inertia to momentum, you experience a completely different dynamic. Have you ever gone into the garage just looking for something on your messy workbench, decided to just straighten up the tools a bit, and ended up two days later having organized the garage, causing your loved ones to discuss mounting an intervention to get you out of the garage? That's the difference between being a victim to inertia, overwhelmed at the idea of a daunting task, and being the beneficiary of momentum and becoming unstoppable.

When I say I have No Matter Watt habits, I'm referring to the very small tasks I give myself to do every day with a sacred commitment to do them every single day No Matter Watt! It is this transfer from stasis to momentum, and from procrastination to unstoppable, which is the key to behavior transformation and being able to accomplish the things in your life that really make a difference.

Speaking of making a difference, one of my No Matter Watt habits is to grab my tray of vitamins and supplements while my first cup of coffee is brewing. I can be relied upon to go to the coffee machine every single morning, so that is the trigger for the mini-habit of pulling my basket of vitamins down, taking one of each of them, and putting them on a plate. That's it. That's the habit. I don't have to take the vitamins, I just have to get one of them onto the plate before my coffee finishes brewing. Of course, once I'm standing there with my cup of coffee in my hand and my plate of vitamins in front me, I've gone about 99% of the way toward hitting my goal of sitting down with my coffee and some water and taking my vitamins every day. One of them happens to be an 81-mg aspirin. My doctor told me that at my age, taking that 81-mg aspirin could add between 10 and 15 years to my life. That's inspiring. Before I learned mini-habits, you could've told me I was going to be dead in a week if I didn't take something every day for seven days, and I would bet against my making it. That's because inspiration works for only a very short period of time. What inspiration is good for is starting a No Matter Watt habit. Now, because of that habit and not because I have discipline, I've been taking that 81-mg aspirin for several years every single day. Who knows what the consequences might have been if I was not able to get myself to do that?

The truth of the matter is that it's nearly impossible to do just one push-up. Every once in a while, I will be heading to bed at about 11:30 and realize that I have not done any exercise. That's when I will jump out of bed, get down on the ground, do one push-up, and then get back in bed. Checkmark. OK, usually I do two or three then. Checkmark. Once you get down on the ground, get your face into the dusty carpet, and get back up to the top of your push-up, you will feel an almost irresistible urge to do one more push-up—If for no other reason than that it would feel silly to do all that and then really do only one push-up. Most of the time you'll knock out 10 or 20, and some days you'll knock out several sets of 20 as you move through an impressive workout and really make significant progress toward your actual goal, which is to be in great shape. Now you've accomplished both the checkmark and the goal. The key is that getting the checkmark is absurdly easy and leads inevitably to the seemingly unattainable goal.

One of my No Matter Watt habits led to a huge breakthrough. Initially, I had a commitment to knock on one door after each appointment and try to get another appointment. This seems like a reasonable enough behavior to get a checkmark every time. However, I found myself over and over again being unable to overcome my resistance to going up to even one door and trying to get an appointment. Stephen Guise says in *Mini Habits* that if you find yourself unable to perform the mini-habit, then you have set the bar too high and it needs to be a lot more absurd. In his new book *Elastic Habits*, he creates a system whereby you can build upon many habits to reach "plus" and "elite" levels of behaviors to incorporate that as part of the structure. But he expounds on the idea that to complete a mini habit, it needs to be so absurdly low that you could accomplish it on the worst day of your life. So I realized that I needed to make my sacred commitment more absurd and set a lower bar than knocking on *one* door. Well, what could be lower than that? It occurred to me that I go to extreme measures to make every interaction end in a yes. That is partly what makes me such a good closer. Well, that same trait was making me a terrible prospector. There is no way around the fact that most doors you knock on will result in a no. My closer mentality experienced that as failure and rejection. I took on that personally by nature, and it was often devastating to my mood and emotional state. No wonder I was avoiding it like the plague. I realized I needed to create a different objective and lower the bar of my No Matter Watt habit. If the result was most often going to be a no, then I needed to make that the objective. I needed to lower the bar so that every day and after every appointment I would have to go to one door and get *one no!* And that is exactly what I did. It became funny to me to find one homeowner, get them to say no, and then come down the driveway high-fiving myself. What also happened is that when I crossed the threshold from 0 to 1, I often found myself getting a yes on that one door! I also found myself in motion with a card in my hand when the next-door neighbor pulled up in the driveway, and it was then effortless to walk up and help them get their groceries in the house.

If the bar is set low enough, it does not matter how late you are for work, how bad a day you're having, or how busy a day you're having; there is no reasonable excuse for not getting the check mark.

Another thing I do every morning is my mastermind the No Matter Watt Club. Napoleon Hill in his book *Think and Grow Rich* explains that the idea of a mastermind is that when two or more minds join each other, a third mind is created; it's a unique entity. That's what brainstorming is all about. You can't brainstorm with yourself, so a brainstorm is a master-mind activity. The sum of the parts of that mastermind group are greater than the whole. That additional mind is a receiver of ideas, energy, infor-mation, events. That's what happens when multiple minds work together toward one definite purpose. All this is to utilize the tools out there in the universe to actually become whatever you want. If that's rich, then be rich. If that's to be a philanthropist, then be a philanthropist.

Also, be ready for what you asked for. When you put your brain to work and it starts working, you're going to wake up in the middle of the night and say, "You know what? If I add this canvassing activity to this part of my schedule here, then I think I will be in three or more appoint-ments a week." Have you ever tried to remember the name of that guy from a movie you couldn't remember? That happens to all of us, right? Try this: tell your brain, "That's cool—we don't know it. But when you get the answer, let me know." Sometime in the next 24 hours, while your brain is doing a Google search, it's going to hit you. If you give your brain a job, it will start working.

In *Think and Grow Rich*, Napoleon Hill quotes the poet Jessie Rittenhouse: "I bargained with Life for a penny, and Life would pay no more, however I begged in the evening when I counted my scanty store. For life is a just employer. He gives you what you ask, But once you have set the wages, Why, you must bear the task. I worked for a menial's hire, Only to learn, dismayed, That any wage I had asked of life, Life would have willingly paid."

So you get to set your rate. You get to decide how much money you're going to make, and if you're making a hundred thousand dollars a year and you think that's awesome, then great. But you get to decide that you can dedicate your energy to making the amount of money you want to make. You're the one who gets to decide what that is, but most of us never understand that. We are the ones who set the bar in our lives. Why do so few people realize their potential then? I believe it is because few of us are even awake. Fewer are aware of our true reality, and even fewer of us care enough about our lives to take control and start living our dreams. When we live in fear, we play small, and that's how things turn out. Give that some thought. You can create your own mastermind. Mine meets every morning at 8:00 am. By 8:30 in the morning, I'm fired up and feel like I've been shot out of a cannon, and I was the worst morning guy on the planet.

(If you're interested in joining me on that call let me know at MOD@ modsalesacademy.com)

All these changes began because I realized I needed to change the way I thought. I don't have a lot of regrets in my life, but one of the things I do regret is that I went through my thirties and forties without figuring out and understanding that I was trying to become financially independent. I didn't realize I should have been trying to figure out how to have a seven-figure income and a nine-figure net worth. And so I spent my thirties and my forties not doing that, thinking that if I made a quarter of a million dollars, paid my bills, put 4 percent in a 401(k) and just didn't fail somehow, then I was being successful.

Once I got a taste of actually performing at my optimal rate, that all changed. You may not want to work the way I work. You may not want to put the amount of time into selling that I do, so you may not want to have a seven-figure income. If you want to make $300,000 or a half a million dollars a year, that's great. If you want to live in Guatemala, measuring your success by how much your nonprofit is improving the nutrition of hyper-low-income families and making $38,000 per year doing that, awesome! Set your goals and wage intentionally and have 1-year, 3-year, 5-year, and 10-year targets for production, income, and net worth.

You have to put your brain to work. One of the problems with our brain is it doesn't have a job. That's why we watch TV. What our brain does primarily when we don't give it something to do is worry and shift into anxiety. I struggle with fear and anxiety every day. So you have to give your brain a job. That's what happened: I started to teach my brain how to think. You do that by reading your daily mantra, which is your chief objective. It's all of your goals, the things you want to accomplish. This is a reprogramming of your brain.

Most of the people we know are very successful at very bad goals. There are people just as passionate about what they do, are good at what they do, and are even recognized for what they do but are making $80,000 a year. Nowhere in their mind are they thinking they should make a half million dollars a year because if they did, they wouldn't be doing what they're doing. Now, if that person decides they want to make $500,000 per year, they need to do something different. They need to stop being successful at a goal they don't desire and start succeeding at a goal that is worthwhile, even if that means potentially failing at first.

I'm not talking from some mountain top. I'm talking about being a guy for whom big meant making $150,000 to 250,000 a year. In my mind, that was successful. But really, it was small and fearful thinking. The idea of taking the leap from a six-figure salary working for corporate America, with the company taking the risk and keeping the lion's share of my efforts, to working for myself as a straight-commission salesman was terrifying. However, taking the leap and betting on myself resulted in not just taking the risk but also getting the lion's share. Changing how I thought changed everything for me.

Chapter 7
Go For No: It's Where the Money Is

When I say that No is where the money comes from I am not being oblique. If most people weren't horrified at the idea of going up to a perfect stranger and asking them to consider buying their product then Sales would pay the same as anything else. It's the fact that most people when asked are going to say no and that some of them may do this very rudely and that most people cannot get themselves to even consider doing this that makes the compensation so lucrative. If a company knew which prospects were going to say yes they would just go directly to those doors with people who are paid on salary and we wouldn't be needed.

My brain had been broken, but I was starting to fix it. I realized that instead of going to the door and trying to get an appointment, I would set the bar absurdly low. I would go to the door after every presentation and try to get someone to tell me "no." How easy is that? How could I convince myself that I wasn't up to knocking on a door and getting someone to say no? This completely changed the game for me.

Being freed up from the idea that I was trying to get someone to say yes and instead being tasked with going to the door and making sure someone was a no was incredibly liberating. It's something I could convince myself to do every single day, between every single appointment.

The title of this book could have been "Get One No". It's the primary ingredient needed to overcome the reason why 100 percent of salespeople aren't as successful as they could be. It's because they all stop prospecting; they all stop knocking on doors. It's something that provokes tremendous resistance, and as a result, even if they have some success with it, they normally end up slowing down and then coming to a full stop. They just cannot make themselves go knock on one more door.

But the exercise is really to get one no because you're making a sacred commitment to do the bare minimum and to get the checkmark ✔ on your No Matter Watt habit. When you transition from not knocking on any doors to knocking on one, it makes all the difference in the world. And not always, but often, it creates the inertia that causes success to happen. People are programmed to have a fear of rejection. Do you remember the seventh-grade dance, when you wanted to ask the pretty girl in your class to dance but were afraid of her saying no? So you didn't? That turned into never asking, which turned into missing out on some yeses because of your fear of no.

It comes back to the math. Let's say for every 12 conversations you have, 11 say no and one says yes. You make $3,000 for a yes. Every no gets you one step closer to the twelfth answer, which is a yes, so what the job pays is $250 for every person that tells you no. The trick is to think, "No? Great! I just made $250!"

When you think about it that way, why not knock on more doors? That's literally what every single salesperson on the planet is not doing 99.99% of the time. And that's simply because getting told no sucks. And it doesn't get any better—trust me, I've been doing this for 40 years. But most people aren't rude. In my experience, maybe one in 20 are rude, with the others being very polite. Most often, when you ask the pretty girl to dance, if she says no, she's nice about it. But there are those mean girls, and it's them we're afraid of 100% of the time. We imagine the worst-case scenario in every possible interaction. And it's cumulative somehow. The longer I do it, the stronger the resistance is and the more I have to use hacks and habits to overcome it. It's hard to remember the 19 polite people. It's why everyone knows successful salespeople make a lot of money. It's not because they're good at getting people to say yes. It's because they are willing to be told no and have found a way to deal with the rejection. The rest are just not willing to undertake or risk it.

Go down one driveway, up the next. Go for no, but hear a yes every time.

Your Brain is Broken—Fix It by Understanding What the Money's For

I cannot tell you what the resistance is all about. Why does my mind think that any consequence would be worth not going up to a door? Why is there any resistance to approaching one door when you can make so much money by doing it? I have not found the answer to that question, but I have found the solution. That solution is turning a mini habit into a No Matter Watt habit.

Instead of using my mind to think, I was using it to worry and fret about any number of things that were just as unlikely to come about. I created a list of things that I wanted to become true and focused on what was to be my main purpose. I set about trying to reprogram my brain, put it to work, and get busy coming up with ideas, plans, and energy to make those specific desires become a reality. My objective is to help between 200 and 300 families a year make a decision to install solar on their home. I train myself to keep my eye on the objective. All this while still going for a "No."

We've all heard it: sales is a numbers game. How you get yourself to do the numbers is a different thing. The key is to understand that this is now a decision. This is not magic. It's not a variable. It's a decision. It's

79

math! If you want to reach your goal, you just have to reverse-engineer how many hours and how many doors and how many conversations it takes to get you there. And it's less than you think. Of course, you then also have to go out and do the appointments, but those aren't the work. When you show up at someone's house and they invite you in and they're glad to see you, you sit down and get to do something cool, which is have a conversation about how awesome your product is, and at the end of it, they sign up. That's a sale, but it really isn't work. The work is to get yourself from where you are currently to being on a door.

The problem is that your brain at that moment does not understand what the money's for. We think that we get paid $1,000 to $5,000 for spending 90 minutes with somebody and getting their name on a piece of paper. You have to understand that is not even remotely close to what the money's for. The money is for the twenty doors you knocked on to get one appointment. Then you had to make three appointments to get one of them closed on average. Those are the numbers. But it took about twenty conversations to get one appointment. Again, three appointments to have one of them close. You have to divide up those 60 homes and those 60 conversations by the $3,000 and understand that that's what the money's for. Now it's not weird anymore. If you figured out that you are getting about fifty dollars to just go knock on that door and be told no, would you do it? For fifty bucks, I would do it.

Hopefully by now you've decided being on doors is worth investing more time. But the more things you decide are more important than do-ing this job on the doors, the less money you're going to make. And the problem with successful salespeople and the best salespeople is that they figure out how to use their talent, their resources, and their cleverness to outsmart this part of the job, and the smarter they are, the faster their income falls.

The reason I'm all about the math is because I know what the money is for: the effort, not the outcome. Most of the effort is your ability to do the work and take the no's, to deal with the rejection. People experience no as rejection. That's normal. If you experience no as rejection, that's normal. But no isn't rejection. No is the answer to a question. We're actually getting paid for all of the effort, which is mostly getting no's. So if you understand and can convince your brain what you're actually being paid for, which is to get told no, then being told no goes from being a tragedy, something we are genetically hardwired to avoid, into a normal part of my job and a prerequisite to making money.

Your brain is broken because it doesn't understand that for every door you knock on, you're getting paid $50, $100, or in my case, $500. By the way, for $500 I still don't want to get out of my truck a lot of the time. Yesterday, I had an appointment and sale in a gated community with homes worth $10 million to $15 million. Afterward, I am looking up and down this street, and it screams money. I am behind the gate by invitation and looking at homes that pay $10,000 plus per year to the utility company, and I want to run and hide. Why? Do I hate money? What was the issue? The issue was fear. It's hard to intimidate me, but I was intimidated. Like brushing my teeth, I just didn't go back to my truck and instead climbed the next-door neighbor's driveway and rang the gong.

What ensued was one of the nicest conversations I've ever had with an extremely polite and cultured lady, who had never had anyone show up on her doorstep and invite her to receive a free, fully engineered solar design projecting $10,000 in savings a year and a $250,000 increase in her cash and equity positions. I don't care how rich you are; you have to admit those numbers should get your attention. Well, they got hers. She was very happy to have me over to show her and her husband a proposal. Oh, and by the way, she was the president of the homeowners' association and was also happy to direct me to several neighbors who she thought would be interested to hear about this. Given that we were facing a tax credit deadline, she asked me to go right away. Within a week I had the original sale and four more enormous systems sold on that street.

I can guarantee you that if I had consulted my brain or feelings I would not have gone anywhere near that 14-foot-tall door.

Going for no is always a great way to save time to get on more doors. Let's say you approach a guy in a garage and start talking to him. He's friendly; he's asking questions. You've been taught previously in sales to make a friend, so that's what you're doing. After 25 minutes, you ask to set up an appointment. But now his whole demeanor changes. He was just lonely. His wife is in charge, and he's not authorized. Now you've wasted all this time.

Compare that to the rude guy who immediately slams the door in your face. I'll take that guy all day. Could that have gotten me down? Sure, but it doesn't. Why? Because I go for no, and I got my no fast. I didn't waste time, and I did my job. Not only that, when I divide the 15 seconds I spent on this door by how much I get paid for a no, I see that this was the most lucrative conversation I had all day.

If you put the time into it and you ask enough people, you're going to end up on the other side with literally hundreds and then thousands of people who have said yes. I've had over a thousand people buy solar from me. That's a lot of times that I had to simply ask somebody, "Will you look at a quote?"

Understanding the mindset that this is an Easter-egg hunt is key. If you figure out how many people you need to talk to before one says yes, you'll know how many Easter eggs you have to pick up to reach your goal. If you treat it like an Easter egg hunt, it's also more fun. I don't care which one has a jelly bean, which one has a chocolate egg and which one has $3,000. The only thing I care about is getting through as many as I can possibly get through.

And if you keep doing it, it will compound. If my entire company knocks on 24,000 doors, our closing rate is 8,000. That's somewhere approximating 8,000 times that we've had somebody say yes as a result of knocking on doors. And none of it was magic. It was 24,000 appointments that turned into 8,000 installations. That's just math. The math produces the results. No is one possible result. Yes just happens to be the result that is the cashier.

It's like a reverse casino. The casino knows they're going to make a certain number of dollars. They aren't the ones gambling. They make that money to the penny. That money comes out in their favor to the exact amount they expected. Why? Because math always works.

Let's continue this gambling scenario. Ever play Texas hold 'em? You get two cards and normally it's something like a nine and a four. You think, "How am I going to win money when they keep dealing me nine-four, queen-three, six-jack? What am I going to do with these? These cards are horrible." Then, boom, you look down at two cards: one of them is an eight, and the other one is an eight. You think, "Whoa, something weird just happened." You got dealt a pair. But you can go for what feels like hours without being dealt a pair.

It turns out you get dealt a pair every 14 times they deal you cards. Now, is it possible to go 28 times in a row without getting a pair? Yes. Is it possible to go a hundred times without getting a pair? That's stretching the bounds of mathematical probability, but it could happen. You could get a hundred hands in a row and not make a pair. And then you look down at a king and a king, an awesome pair! It seems like magic! But over the next hundred hands, instead of one out of 14, you're probably going to see two out of 14. Why? Because the math owes you. The math always delivers. And by the way, the math will deliver you pocket kings or pocket aces every 221 deals.

It turns out that every eight times that you do have a pair in Texas hold 'em, one of the next three cards that come out (the flop or community cards) will match the two in your hand, giving you three of a kind! This is called flopping a set, and most times that this happens you will want to "go all in." In most cases, the odds (the math) will be in your favor to win big!

If you put in the work, the math will provide for you. If you find out what your yeses per conversation are, the math will reward you. It will pay you. You just have to get yourself to crank the numbers. That's why the casino is offering you a free lobster dinner. They need you in there. They'll give you whatever it takes as long as you'll be part of the math because the math works out in their favor.

Knocking on doors can be brutal. Knowing that math is in your favor and never fails will turn each no into just one of the results you get paid very well for. Understanding this and experiencing the money go into my pocket with each no was extremely liberating. It made the effort fun. However, you cannot just snap your fingers and internalize this. In fact, that understanding disappears all the time and is replaced by stinking thinking. I will talk later about the many benefits of showing others how to do this. The only thing I have found that combats the tendency of my mind to fight me is to take someone out and show them how to sell, explaining, demonstrating and yes even preaching this concept as we walk down the driveway of someone who just said no.

Justin Knutson is one of my team leaders and an absolute dynamo on the doors and in the house. He is one of numerous people that have come to SunSolar Solutions to learn how to create a seven-figure income selling solar. He along with his partner Michael Schmeltzer, who discovered our program a few months before he did and encouraged him to stop what he was doing in Oregon and move to Arizona, both won Golden Door awards and achieved very high six-figure incomes in their very first year. He and I were knocking a street right after an appointment. This entailed jumping out of my truck in front of a house with an open garage door while leaving it running. We knocked on the door and the homeowner came to greet us. He looked at the SunSolar logos on our shirts and at the running SunSolar-wrapped Ford F-150 behind me and said, "Solar? F— solar, man!" Instead of being taken aback, having our feelings hurt, or trying to argue with the gentleman, I realized we had achieved our entire objective in about five seconds at this homeowner's door. I looked at him and said, "Sir, it's our job to come up to a door and find out if you're open-minded about solar or not. We've discovered the answer at your door in less time than at any door this week, which is a very success-ful outcome for us. I want to thank you for coming to the door because when people don't, it makes our job impossible to do. Have a great day." The homeowner actually tried to revise his previous statement to soften what he had said and I stopped him. I said, "Listen, we really just want to know if you're interested in a solar quote. It's clear you're not, and we really appreciate your directness. Have a great day!" We turned on our heels, and as we were walking down the driveway we high-fived each other for a job extremely well done. The momentum coming from that driveway propelled us around the cul-de-sac and three doors later to an excellent appointment.

The Worst Kind of No: Cancellations

Keep in mind, cancellations are part of the numbers, so don't let that get you down. Do what you can to follow up so you can minimize the number of times that happens. Many people experience fear and doubt in the day or two after a major purchase. Not only is this a thing, but it has a name: buyer's remorse. Employ vigorous follow-up in the first 24 or 48 hours, and they're less likely to cancel. At SunSolar Solutions we actually employ a platoon of people we call project coordinators to make this call the morning after the sale and to follow up dozens more times between the sale and the installation. We do this so that salespeople do not get bogged down by any tasks other than setting appointments and closing sales. The project coordinator is going to be someone who's really good at follow-up. I'm not good at follow-up. I'm always thinking about who hasn't bought yet, and all of my time, attention, and energy is focused on who is next. Many salespeople get into a mode where they're spending 80 to 90 percent of their time in follow up. I suggest you work for a company that has this support or hire someone yourself to do this work. Your time should be spent on the extremely high-value tasks of setting and closing appointments.

I have a No Matter Watt habit to minimize cancellations: I leave that customer a text message with a voice or video clip in it within minutes or hours of leaving the house. My goal, as my friend Taylor McCathy from Knockstars says, is to get on an emoji-level relationship with them in their text thread. Another No Matter Watt habit is to spend two or three minutes the next day making a 30-second video clip designed to transfer the confidence and conviction I have about the wisdom of their decision and transmit that to them anew. Sometimes I will have a gut feeling that a brand new customer will be feeling shaky the next day. I own the sales, so I make it a habit to show up the next day with a gift of a pie or a house plant with a nice card saying thank you. It gives me an opportunity to show up at their door and thank them while asking if they've had any additional questions come up. If they're wavering, it gives me an opportunity to reinforce the reasons they decided to move forward. This, combined with the work a project coordinator should do, reduces my cancellation rate from the industry average of 40 percent to between 10 percent and 20 percent. No matter what you do in my industry, you're going to experience at least a 10-percent cancellation rate.

Again, devastating, but pick yourself back up by saying you know it's part of the numbers and that you did what you could.

If you do get a cancellation, the most important thing is not to call the person but actually to go right back to their house. You want to do this within an hour of their canceling. Say something like, "Hey, you know what? I was around the corner with your neighbors, and I heard you'd called the office and had some concerns. I was right nearby. So I wanted to make myself available to address those concerns."

It's surprising and even unsettling for some people, but I'm a door guy. I met them by knocking on their door, and so if there's an issue, I'm back at their door. Still, that doesn't work very often. You can save maybe 10 to 25 percent of people who decide to cancel. So, if they are still canceled after you visit, take that as a no and move on! Put them into a bin where you revisit them on a quarterly basis, but get them off your day-to-day task list.

Part 3

7-Figure Prospecting

Chapter 8
Making Appointments

The majority of sales that I make on an annual basis is from knocking doors. When you buy appointments, you're admitting that you're just too lazy to do your own work, and you're spending hundreds of dollars for a bad appointment most of the time because those are all shoppers. When you buy a lead from someone, they have responded to online marketing. The guy that sold me the lead probably sold it to four other people even though he said it was exclusive.

In contrast to that, when you get off your ass to go knock doors, you're talking to someone who is only talking to you about your product. You planted the idea and you are the be-all and end-all, the only person they know in your business. There is a world of difference in that. If you want to run around, wasting a bunch of time, spending all kinds of money, and talking to people who are talking to four or five other companies, then that's the right method for you. If you want to present to somebody who thinks you invented fire and you are the only one they are talking to, then get off your ass and go knock some doors.

As I've shown you in the last chapter, knocking on doors is the best-paying job on the planet. I make more money than most brain surgeons, and I didn't have to go through eight years of school and another eight years of residency and work as a slave for eight years trying to get to this level where I can make a very high six-figure or even seven-figure income. But if it's the simplest and best paying thing you can do and you don't need any credentials or experience, why is it almost impossible to get yourself or anyone else to do it?

I can't tell you how many times I've been in my truck and could not muster the courage to get out and knock on a door. How do you overcome fear? How do the guys in the military get people to charge into the line of live fire? They train them to take the first step, and they teach them how to make the next step. That's how they get people to march into a field of bullets.

Of course, we cannot compare ourselves to what first responders do or people in the military do. There is nothing compared to that. I don't know that fear, but I know the fear of walking up to the first cold door. And I know it's almost impossible to overcome. Everyone feels it, so there's nothing to be ashamed about. But understand you have to overcome that.

Now, I don't have to knock on 20 doors to get one appointment. I knock on about seven doors to get one person to say, "Yeah, I guess it does make sense to look at a free design proposal that could increase my net worth by $100,000." Also, I don't close one out of three, I close three out of four. So that's going to change my math. I make approximately $500 for every door that someone answers and says, "No, I prefer to stay ignorant about how I could improve my net worth by $100,000." Imagine we are sitting in my truck together, and we see a guy watering his bushes with a hose. I say, "I will give you a $100 bill right now if you will hop out and get that guy to say, "No, I don't want a free proposal." Would you do it? Of course you would. I would be willing to bet that you could not get yourself to refuse. For some reason our brain is broken and doesn't connect what the money is actually for. Viscerally experiencing making the money when someone says no is the key turning in the lock. I'm saying this again because it will liberate you from fear.

Can you imagine how horrible I would have felt if I had left that neighborhood and gotten to the other side of that gate without getting one no? Because I did that, I knocked on five or six multi-million-dollar homes and got first one and then several appointments. I just need one appointment from every appointment I go on and I will be perpetually in appointments.

That is my No Matter Watt habit: after every appointment, I'm not allowed back in the truck until I get one no. Once I get back in my truck, the odds of me knocking on even one door drop in half. So I'm not allowed back in my truck. I keep my bag on my shoulder. I've got my iPad in my bag. I don't look like a door-to-door canvasser. I look like a guy showing up to your house for an important appointment.

It's not magic. It's math. It takes me seven conversations. You need to figure out what your numbers are. Knock on doors and start keeping track to figure it out. That math is going to tell you how many appointments you need each year to reach your sales goal. Divide that number by 52: that's how many appointments you need to be in per week. Focus on how many appointments you need per week or even per day, but the schedule changes from day to day. In my experience, I know that I need to be in about fourteen appointments every week. That's two appointments a day, seven days a week for me.

Not everyone is going to want to work seven days a week. When that net-metering deadline was 100 days away, did I take days off? No. When I'm in no-deadline mode, I usually try to take Sundays off. But when I have 100 days left and every one of those days is worth five to ten thousand dollars a piece, do I take Sundays off? No way. And I'm an undisciplined, lazy kind of guy. But if you can get in touch with the urgency that is appropriate to the opportunity, you're going to perceive time as a perishable commodity and make decisions based on what is truly valuable enough to justify forgoing that kind of income. You will find yourself making different decisions about how to schedule your day and week. If you're on track to make $1 million in a year, you still need to take a few days off, but you also need to realize that those days off are costing you approximately $2,700 apiece. Understanding what those days off are worth will help you to make decisions about what is truly worth spending time on.

Every three appointments that you're in that you close can literally change the trajectory of your financial situation. How different will things be if you can pay for your house or pay off your mortgage at the end of a three-month period? You're going to change your whole life. Do you need Sunday off? If you were on that field that we talked about in a previous chapter with the Easter eggs, would you be wondering when your next Starbucks break was going to be?

My coach and mentor, Coach Michael Burt, likes to say, "you don't need more money; you need more people." The people have the money. You're not trying to knock on doors, you're trying to talk to people. The reason you're knocking on doors is the people who are on the other side of the doors.

My good friend, the CEO of D2D Experts and the catalyst for this book, loves to point out to us that everything in life you could possibly need is behind a door. So what can we do to bring the number of doors we get to and the number of conversations with people up to where they need to be to achieve the results we dream of?

I don't knock on doors for four hours a day, or eight hours a day. I knock on doors for an hour to two hours each day. Why? Because I'm in appointments all day. I only have about one to two hours a day total between appointments. I'm knocking on doors for about 25 minutes at a time in between two, three, or four appointments a day. The last thing I want to do is knock on doors for 25 minutes and have people not answer. So when I'm in a neighborhood, I need five or six no's before I get to my next appointment. I don't care how late I am to my next appointment, I'm going to get at least one person to say no.

How am I going to get one no with one attempt. I look for people that are home. If I only have 25 minutes, I have to find people I know are home. Open garage doors are my primary target. I'm looking for a house with three cars in front of it. If I get to seven or eight answered doors between each appointment, I will have set two or three appointments a day. That's the math. Just create the No Matter Watt habits that will generate the math.

This is what that looks like: I see a home with three or four cars in the driveway, an open door in front of a closed screen door, an open garage door, or anything that tells me there are signs of life and people are likely home. Many people don't like to knock on doors at night after dark. It's actually the best time and I love it because I can tell exactly who is home and who is not. I pull over with one wheel on the sidewalk, swing open the door and leave it open with the engine running as I run up to the door and knock, not ring, like the police are at the door. When the homeowner opens the door, they find a businessman on their doorstep who is practically frantic. Why am I frantic? The situation is dire and I have very little time right now, but after missing them several times, I noticed that they were home and I couldn't leave the neighborhood without stopping. I only have a minute. I have to go but I didn't want to miss you, seeing that you're home.

Do not listen to your brain or your feelings that say, "I am too busy. I am too tired. I don't have time." None of those excuses hold up. As Stephen Guise, the author of Mini Habits, says, "Get your face in the carpet and do one push-up." That's what the "Get one no between every appointment is what a No Matter Watt habit is about. Get from zero to one between every single appointment. Stop being the victim of inertia and start being the beneficiary of momentum by getting one no.

Chapter 9
The Hacks and Magic of 7-Figure Prospecting

Show Someone Else

Now let's add some gasoline to the fire you've got started. One of my most important hacks is to always have someone with me showing them how to make money in sales. When I first started in solar, that was my daughter Katherine. She would come and knock on doors with me, learning how to do it. I would then go to appointments, and she would keep knocking on doors. I would pay her part of the commission from each sale that came from every appointment she set. She was the first person that was added to my 1099 company in addition to me. Have your recruit meet you and go with you; that's the hack. When I'm showing somebody else how to knock on doors, the one who is knocking on doors is me. Constantly be showing somebody. Tell them how much money you're making in sales. Consider how many people can no longer live the life they want or even the life they have due to the monstrous jump in home, energy, food, cars, etc., due to the post-covid 7.9-percent inflation. There are a lot of people right now who are looking for a way to make much more money than they were before. This is the perfect opportunity for you to show someone a way to make a fantastic income and for you to grow your business.

Tell your relatives. My daughter, sister and my niece have all knocked on doors with me. They've all made terrific money working a summer, part time or full time knocking on doors. I would say three quarters of the people that I've taken with me have not worked out. Some of them never ended up knocking a single door by themselves. This job is *not* for most people. Don't be discouraged; if they work out, it is just a bonus. The primary objective is to be out yourself knocking on doors, which is going to happen 100 percent of the time you schedule with someone to show them how to do it. Cool things happen when you do this. Number one: you are not at your house on the couch. Number two: because they are with you, you're going to show up and show off. You're going to charge up the driveway, knock on that first door, knock on that second door. Bottom line: while showing off, you will invariably make an appointment. I almost never get skunked when I'm out with someone. I always give the appointment-setting commission, usually $500 to $1,000 to the new recruit even though all they did was watch. There is a better-than-good chance I would not have been on that door if they did not agree to go out with me. Also, that money will whet their appetite for more. Most people have never made $500 to $1,000 doing anything for just a couple of hours. It will be an awakening.

I've been in corporate sales for a long time. My partner Troy Dinbokowitz drove a bread truck and spent all day loading shelves with bread. But he was good at getting the guys to order more donuts and bread, and he was a good sales guy. A friend of his who was knocking on doors in the security industry suggested he come out with him for a couple days to see if direct sales was something he might be interested in. His friend offered to show him how to make three or four times as much money as he'd been making for his family, and Troy jumped at the chance. He stuck with it and had a great career in security sales which led to him getting into solar and eventually starting SunSolar Solutions. He went from a guy supporting his family driving a bread truck to being a seven-figure sales guy and business owner. Never underestimate how badly somebody would like to have an opportunity that really does have the potential to change his or her life. Never underestimate how miserable somebody is doing what they're currently doing and making the money that they're currently making.

This is the most important hack because it's not only helping you, it is helping someone else. You never know.

I'd like to tell you I'm an altruistic guy. I kind of am. But as long as it's helping somebody, while I'm in the process of getting what I want, I'm much more helpful. What I want is more appointments. If you can take people with you and show them how you do it, it's appointments for you and paid training for them. You're training them to just go out and talk to people and get them to take a look at a free design proposal. Just see if their house is a good candidate for solar. If you make the sale, then they get a cut.

I've done this for years. I've always had at least one to three people who are knocking on doors with me. I am always showing someone new how to do it. If they knock on doors 15 to 20 hours a week, they should find no less than five to ten people who are interested in looking, and with modest closing percentages they will end up with two or three sales. This would be making $1,500-$3,000 a week working part time. Not a bad gig. People who dedicate themselves to this job can find themselves with five-figure weekly paychecks and a healthy six figure income. It's one of my goals that in the near future we will have succeeded in creating seven-figure appointment setters. Sarah Blomfield moved to Phoenix from Puerto Vallarta, Mexico, to join SunSolar and is known as the "Six-Figure Setter." She has a vision and an Instagram handle reserved for when she makes it to Seven-Figure Setter.

The real issue is that if I am trying to be out there by myself I am going to be in a different mode. I am easily distracted; I might get on social media. I might get discouraged. But if you're with me, I'm going to show off and act like I'm freaking Superman.

My son Joseph is in the company in the marketing department. We call it digital door knocking. He started out with me knocking on doors. One day we were together, and I was visiting a customer whose house I had put a $70,000 solar system on. The neighbor across the street was in his front yard. That's a mandatory conversation. Joseph and I walked up to him and started a conversation about solar and whether or not he would be interested in seeing a free design proposal. He looked at me with absolute disgust that some door-to-door peddler would be talking to him, made some dismissive noise and said, "Dude! I'm in finance. You and I both know that solar doesn't have a decent ROI." Now, I could've stood and argued with this person because he absolutely had no idea what he was talking about. Most people never make even a single dollar of investment into solar. They just redirect their monthly energy cost away from being a renter of the power company's equipment, which has an ever-increasing variable cost, to being an owner of their own equipment, which not only never goes up but actually costs significantly less than they are currently spending, thereby creating a positive cash flow on a zero investment. (By the way, if you missed it, that is the pitch). Those misconceptions come from ignorance, and it's part of my job to educate and overcome ignorance. However, it's not part of my job to be shamed especially in front of my son by someone that is rude. So instead of trying to be of service, I thanked the man for his patience and wished him a good day. Now if I had been by myself and had been subjected to that kind of condescension, I may have found myself on my ass and back in my truck headed to Starbucks. But because I was showing off, I said to my son, "Let me tell you how we respond when somebody is a jerk." We promptly walked up the driveway of his next-door neighbor, pointed to the home across the street, and told the neighbor about the family we had just helped. We set an appointment that led to another $70,000 solar sale with another of his neighbors, whom we educated and who will end up with a multiple-six-figure increase in his net worth on account of owning a power plant. I am sure Finance Guy is still experiencing unspoken doubt about what these people know that he doesn't.

I am constantly recruiting people to do this. And I have found out I have made so many more sales on appointments that I set showing people how to do it than I have from anything else.

If you are a 1099 salesperson, you are an enterprise. Grow your business by adding one more person to your business today. Become a recruiter.

Neighborhood Stalker

If you're by yourself, get into the neighborhood, and if you can't get yourself to knock on doors, that's OK. Here's another hack: be a stalker! Just go sit in the neighborhood and park by the mailbox. Play on your phone, listen to music, do whatever; just have a rule that when somebody comes to the mailbox, you're going to follow them home. You're going to stalk them. Give them a few minutes to get settled and then go knock on that door. Better yet, park two houses away and come up on them in their driveway "by chance." Now what do you have? One knock, one person at home, and one conversation every time: one perfect chance to get one no.

If you go to an appointment and you don't want to knock on a door afterwards, use this hack: get in your car, but don't leave. Stay in the neighborhood; all of the money is in the neighborhood. Stay where the money is. Sit on your ass, but if someone pulls up in their driveway, you go knock on that door. Position yourself so you can see the whole street, where you can see 15 to 20 homes. When you see someone pulling up to their driveway, you're going to let them get in the house. Or again, if you're feeling a little ballsy, then go right up to them as they are pulling up. I will literally follow them home and park my big SunSolar truck behind them, with one wheel on the curb and leave my truck door open and say, "Hey folks, I noticed you pulling up, and I have been trying to catch you at home, we are in the process of putting solar up for several of your neighbors. I only have a minute right now and can't stay, but let me just give you one of my cards."

Cherry picking is when you go out and find people who are home. The enemy of knocking on doors is not no it's no one home. So the first thing I do is talk to all the people I can tell are home—where their front doors are open, their garage doors open, they're in the driveway, they're doing yard work—where I can see them or see definite signs of life. I'll get five or six of those, guaranteed, in a neighborhood. Then I could either start knocking on the rest of the doors, or go to the next neighborhood and cherry-pick there. The second option is actually better.

Knocking in the Dark (The It's Too Late Hack)

Many reps feel uncomfortable knocking after the sun goes down. They feel like it's too late. The opposite is actually true. Most people are not home during the day and you cannot speak to them at their door. It does feel a little uncomfortable walking up to a door in the dark and ringing the bell or knocking. What you need to remember is that it is not dark on the other side of the door. Step back, look professional, and give a friendly greeting. Let them know you were just visiting with one of their neighbors and have not been able to catch them in but noticed that they were home. If someone does make a comment about it being awfully late, remind them that since your job is to be meeting the homeowners in this neighborhood when they're home, we have to work when they are off, which means nights and weekends. It's very difficult to be annoyed with someone who is doing their job. Especially one they know would be terrifying to them. Sometimes I'll make a joke and say that my boss is a real jerk and doesn't let me quit for the day until I've made three appointments in the neighborhood. I've already got two, and if you guys will agree to have us come and show you a free solar proposal I'll be done for the night and get to go home!

The "It Really is Too Late to Knock" Hack

Remember my No Matter Watt habit of getting one now after every appointment. A lot of my appointments don't end till after 9 o'clock and sometimes as late as 10:30 at night. How in the world am I going to get a no when it really is too late to knock on doors. Simple! I promise you if you drive around a neighborhood at this time of night, you will find somebody walking their dog or working on a project in their garage. I love to roll up to somebody walking their dog and roll my window down and say hello. I asked them if they are one of the homeowners in the neighborhood. That's a very specific question and elicits a specific answer. Usually the answer is yes. And then I explained I just finished up with one of their neighbors for a solar proposal and I was curious if they've had one done for their home yet? This is not a high-percentage play and usually leads to a polite "No thank you," at which point I am ecstatic to have gotten a no and to be on my way home with a check mark. But you never know. I have several encounters a year like this where the person says, "Funny you should ask. We're actually looking at solar right now."

The guy working on the project in the garage at that time of night is by definition lonely and very often is glad to have a brief, friendly conversation. Sometimes it's hard to get away from these guys once the conversation starts. No matter how it goes, there's no chance you're not going to walk up the driveway and at least have a guaranteed no!

The "They Already Have It" Hack
If you are not up for talking to a prospect, then knock on the door of someone that already owns the product. I love to roll into a neighborhood and knock on one or two doors of people that already have solar. They have zero sales resistance and love to talk about their excellent decision. This will accomplish several things. It will break the inertia of knocking and talking. I like to make them honorary customers and tell them about our referral program as many will have lost touch with their salesperson and company most of the time. I sometimes get a referral right on the spot. But the real benefit is that it will give a real encounter and a neighbor's name to mention at all the other doors on the street. "Do you know Shirley Wood? Lives three houses down. They have the fountain in their front yard. We were just comparing her experience and cost for energy since going solar, and...." Also, they may tell you that their system is grossly undersized and that they would like a quote for more solar!

How to Knock

As of this writing, we are still in the midst of the Covid-19 pandemic. This is not an excuse to not knock on doors. If the virus is hot, find a place to leave a card somewhere near the door. Leave it in the screen door, on a window sill, on a bench, knock on the door and ring the bell and then literally back up like twelve feet. When they answer the door, keep your distance, give them a friendly wave, and let them start the conversation. Let them set the distance that is comfortable to them for the interaction.

By the way, don't just ring a doorbell and wait. Knock like the police are at the door. If you don't hear something in the next ten seconds, knock on the door again and ring the doorbell. Why do I do that? I was with my sister one day, and a couple of her kids and one of her grandsons were there. We were all at the kitchen counter, and we heard "ding dong!" Her four-year-old grandson announces "Amazon!" Nobody looked up or moved towards the door. Why do you think that is? Why would a whole household hear a doorbell and not move a muscle? Then her grandson again says "Amazon!" Today, nine times out of ten, when a door bell rings, it's Amazon, Fedex or UPS leaving a package; it's not someone at the door. After going to the door dozens of times and finding no one there, people learn to ignore it. When I knock on the door, I want there to be no mistake that someone is at the door waiting.

The Magic

OK, there is some actual magic. It helps to wear a t-shirt that says, "Get off your ass and knock on doors." I have that posted to my mirror and my office wall as a motto. I got that saying from *Bosch*, a TV show about a Los Angeles homicide detective. In his little cubicle at the LAPD headquarters, he has this motto tacked to his cubicle wall. Police also have to get into the neighborhood, knock on doors, and talk to people.

When I show someone how to canvas a neighborhood, I keep a magic stone and 30 business cards in the left pocket. I keep 30 sunflower seeds—exactly—in the right pocket. When you go to a door, knock with your magic rock. It *will* sound like the police are at the door. A pest-control professional taught me this. She told me that you always want to carry a magic stone with you so that you don't end up destroying your knuckles.

OK, here's the magic formula. Go to one door with the magic stone in your left hand and a business card in your right hand. After rapping on the door frame with the stone, which will cause the sound to go through the entire house, you wait for the homeowner. When they come to the door, flick the business card with your thumb and hold it out. It's almost impossible to resist the urge to not be rude, and they will open the door. As they do, step out and back so that they have to close the screen door behind them and take the card from you. You're going to have a conversation with them. At some point, propose the idea to come back with an engineer-designed solar proposal they can use to determine whether their house is crappy or awesome for solar. The numbers will tell them, not you. The proposal will include the exact amount of money that the federal government will be contributing to the project via a tax credit as well as any state or local incentives. It will also show them what the projected cost to do nothing and stay with the utility company will be over the next 10, 20, and 25 years. It will show them what investment is needed upfront, which in most cases is literally zero. It will also show them what their monthly positive cash flow or profit will be each month because they switched to solar. There's no obligation or charge for the design proposal, and you'll be leaving that with them so they can think about it and determine whether they want to stay with the utility or convert to solar. Finally, the design proposal will show them the increase in their net worth (their total wealth). That will most certainly be a result of switching from the power company to owning their own power plant.

Your objective is not to get them to say yes; it's to get them to say either no or yes. In either event, your mission is to get a business card carried by them into their home. Also, whether they say yes or no, you're going to take one of the 30 sunflower seeds out of your pocket and toss it into their yard as you walk to the next house. Here's the magic part: if you get 30 business cards into 30 homes and 30 sunflower seeds out of your pocket into 30 yards, at the end of that time, you will almost certainly have at least one, if not two or three appointments, each one having the potential to generate thousands of dollars in income. My partner Troy taught me this amazing magic trick, and it really works! Or is it math?

$100 Bills in Your Pocket

Try this. Keep $2,000 in $100 bills in your pocket. Because my hobby is Texas hold 'em poker, this is normal to me, but you may have to go to the bank. Pay yourself physically. Every time you get to a door and get a no, take a $100 bill out of your roll and put it in your wallet. By getting out a $100 bill and paying yourself, you'll start associating a no with something awesome, not something that sucks. You'd be excited to get a no if I told you I would hand you $100 for going to a door and getting one, right? And here's the thing: this is actually happening! You really do make that much or hopefully more. Make this transformation and you will hit warp speed.

The Best Day to Knock on Doors

Friday is the best day to knock on doors. I say it because a lot of sales-people are tempted to take it off and take a long weekend. It's not a great day for appointments anyway because people are often in a good mood, so they will want to go out and will cancel on you. For the same reason, however, it's a great day to knock on doors from the afternoon until early evening.

Why is it the best day? Because many people leave the office early to get an early start on the weekend, so they're home a little earlier. For many, it's also payday, which puts some money in their pockets and a bounce in their step. They're also looking forward to their plans for the night and the weekend. Bottom line: they're going to be in a pretty good mood and feeling optimistic about the future.

On the other hand, it's also true that Saturday is the very best day. That's because people are typically off work and home that day. They're in a chill mood and have a little more time than they do on a normal work-day. If you're in a neighborhood at 9:30 am on a Saturday, you won't even have to knock on doors. You'll be able to find enough people in their yards doing yard work and relaxing, which is the perfect opportunity to approach them and introduce yourself.

Then again, Sunday is actually the very best day because everyone is at home. And that's the best-kept secret. Nobody knocks on Sundays; people feel hesitant about it because they feel like they're intruding on somebody's peace and quiet. The customer might feel that way, but I'd say eight times out of ten they don't feel that way. It's because they're relaxed. They just had a nice weekend. Maybe they're arriving back from church, and they feel like they need to be good and smile at you. It really is the best day because you will find people are at home, door after door after door.

The magical effect of experiencing a no as a positive revenue event instead of as a tragedy doesn't come into full bloom until you start giving that concept away to others. Once you share this idea with someone else is when it becomes an actual experience. It wasn't until I started talking about it and teaching it to people that I actually felt richer after being on a door and being told no.

I've devoted a lot of thought and practice over the years to overcoming the cause of this internal resistance. Progress came when I started to really break down the psychological effects of rejection and understand how embarrassment, shame, anger, and fear paralyze a person. The effects can be cumulative over time. You may start out lighthearted and become more and more weighed down over time. I have had numerous reps who were very successful for extended periods of time but became increasingly overpowered until they came to a complete stop and could not knock on one more door. They developed a physical revulsion at the idea of experiencing more of the emotions that came with the rejection.

I have thought about trying to use hypnotherapy or some other means of altering the reptilian brain so that the salesperson couldn't care less and was completely detached. But "go for no" goes far beyond that. You're conditioning your brain to experience rejection not as a cataclysmic tragedy, but as a positive revenue event. In fact, the reason we're being paid so much is because of the no's and because so few people are able to deal with them. Paying yourself for each no turns each one into an event to be celebrated.

I have experienced this transformation from dread to excitement for myself and have seen it firsthand every day in the people on my team.

Chapter 10
How to Get a Yes on the Door: "I've Got to Go"

Everyone wants to know: What do I say when they actually get to the door and open it? The answer is simple: it doesn't really matter what you say when they open the door. You're gonna say some stuff, and they're gonna say some stuff. You can say some version of, "You wouldn't be interested in a quote, would you?" Some will, some won't. You're going for a no so that you can keep knocking on doors until you think you're done—and then do one more door.

Often we don't knock on the first door of the day because we just don't feel like we got our mouth wrapped around the pitch. It really doesn't matter. The worst pitch is the best pitch if it's the one you actually end up doing at the door.

Whatever you do, bring some urgency to the door. Let them know you're in a rush too. It gives them the sense that you won't waste your own time and that you're in demand. I actually say, "I have to go," or " I only have a minute" as soon as they open the door. I'm communicating that my time is scarce and that I don't have the ability to spend 20 minutes taking up their time. I'm not trying to get a major credit card or get into their home. Literally, I have to go.

Why would my first and primary message be when someone answers the door that "I have to go"? When someone looks out their window and sees someone with a lanyard around their neck and an iPad in their hands, their first thought is, crap, it's a salesperson. They're going to take up the next half hour of my time, trying to get their foot in the door and get me to give them a major credit card.

When they open the door and find a business person with nothing in their hands but a business card and our hearing and seeing that this person really needs to get going, it completely interrupts their normal resistance patterns.

So when I knock on the door, I say, "Hi there. I was just with your neighbors, the Joneses—you know, the ones with the blue station wagon, all the kids, and the crazy Christmas lights every year? Anyway, they're going solar with us. I noticed you were home. I don't have any time today, but I just wanted to drop off a card. I only have a minute."

That's how I tell them I have to go. "I'm here to drop off a card, and I only have a minute." And I'm going to keep my promise. I'm going to be gone in literally a single-digit number of minutes because I'm not going to give them an entire presentation at the door. "I am going to be leaving shortly but I can come back and give you much more information about why so many of your neighbors are going solar."

By the way, notice how I referred to one of their neighbors. It doesn't matter if they know them or not (no one knows their neighbors), but if you can refer to another neighbor you had a conversation with, that puts them at ease and also makes them want to be in the know. Hopefully they will join the "bandwagon."

After I tell them I have to go, I'm going to ask them a question and then shut up. This also puts them off guard because they're expecting you to launch into a pitch and that they will have trouble getting you to shut up. Now we've told them we have to go and are inviting them to talk. It doesn't matter what the question is. I like this one: "Have you put any thought into...?" And then you fill in the blank with your product. I may also ask them if my company has given them their free solar design yet. "Have you had a design done for your home already?"

The purpose of this question is to give me a reason to shut up and listen. The customer is about to reveal their pre-existing thoughts, interest, objections and maybe even complete revulsion to your product or being approached about any product. It may lead to the discovery of a complete Easter egg.

The other morning on one of the 8 o'clock calls, one of my sales people talked about going to a door with someone he's training the day before. They knocked at the house at 11 o'clock in the morning. The homeowner opened the door and asked them to come in. He invited them to have a seat at the kitchen table. They were already wondering what was going on when the homeowner asked if they had the proposal ready? He told them he had come by to see if he would like to get a proposal and that he would be happy to go to the engineering department and have one prepared. The homeowner was confused and said that he had an appointment at 11 o'clock for a solar person to show up and go over the proposal he had asked for the day before. He explained that they had just come to his door to introduce themselves and that it must've been another solar company. They proceeded to talk about the solar solution and answered many of his questions. He said that he didn't know what had happened to the other company but since they had failed to show up for the appointment he was interested in having them provide a proposal instead. As they were leaving they met a representative from the other solar company coming up the walk. The homeowner told him that he was not happy that he was late for the appointment and that he was going to be going solar with our company. Those don't come along too often but it fits one of my favorite sayings: the harder you work the luckier you get!

Most of the time the prospect will respond to the question with either ambivalence, disinterest or perhaps some kind of a brush off. You may also get some useful clues to their disposition and use that to give you an idea how to frame the rest of the conversation. At this point, I'm going to bring up several big ideas that have the ability to generate substantial interesting benefits. I am going to follow that up with points of urgency and ask the customer if they're aware of the critical nature that faces them. My objective is to say several things that will appeal to the prospect in a powerful way.

I will typically say something like, "Our design proposal would tell you exactly how much money the federal government would be Investing into your home. Typically on a home this size, the federal subsidy is between $10,000 and $14,000. That would likely come to you next spring when you do your taxes. It would also tell you how much you would be receiving from the state incentive program. Of course solar energy is absolutely free but the equipment is not. If you qualify for our program it actually has zero upfront cost, would cause your current electric bill to all but go away and provide you with a monthly payment that is significantly less than you're paying the utility for their power which is essentially renting their equipment. The proposal would show you what the positive cash flow would be in your first month and what the profit would be in year one as well as over 10 and 20 years. Most of our customers experience a total profit of over $100,000 switching from the fossil fuel product of the local utility monopoly to ownership of their own renewable energy solar power plant."

I will immediately follow that up with a question that goes to the urgency of their situation:

"Did you see that President Biden's Build Back Better plan has been stopped in Congress and that this is the last year the federal government is offering the 26% tax credit?"

"Have you been following in the newspaper about your utility company's proposal being accepted by the state and that the current Solar Export Credit System is coming to an end at the end of the summer?"

"Most families purchase their solar power plants with $0 down long-term financing agreements. Did you see that the Fed is projecting five or six interest rate hikes this year which will increase the cost of solar along with all energy?"

"Did you see that the Congress passed the $1.9 trillion infrastructure bill and that one of the ways that it's going to be paid for is by increasing taxes on the fossil fuels being used to generate your electricity?"

"Did you see that the United States has stopped the construction of the Keystone XL pipeline and re-entered the Paris climate accord as part of our nation's plan to get serious about climate change and kick off the Green New Deal?"

These issues are not gimmicks. They are very real local, national, and global issues that are having and will continue to have a dramatic effect on what homeowners pay for energy. These are the reasons that you are so busy and that you are at their door somewhat frantic. If they are comprehending what you're talking about, this frantic state will be contagious.

I knocked on a gentleman's door several days after the United States banned the import of Russian oil due to the Ukrainian war. He told me that he had looked at Solar when he moved in three years ago and that he didn't see an adequate return on investment. I asked him if he had been paying attention to what was going on in the news about Russian oil. He told me that I had actually interrupted him executing trades on oil futures. I responded by remarking about how oil was now $100 a barrel. He said that I must be out of the loop for several hours because it hadn't been $100 a barrel since this morning. It was currently trading at $107 a barrel and he was dealing with futures contracts that were putting oil at $135 a barrel in the very near future. In my pivot back to solar, I pointed out that while I thought solar would have a phenomenal return on investment, that was irrelevant. The primary objective in installing a solar plant was to lock in the price of your family's fuel for the next 30 years. He said, "You're right. Get me the numbers." That entire conversation took less than five minutes.

This powerful one-two punch of big picture benefits coupled with issues they are powerless over that will both increase the cost of their current fossil fuel energy supply and reduce benefits and subsidies of solar will cause the urgency needed to drop the pretext that this is not worth their time or attention.

Do not make the mistake of thinking that the primary benefit of solar is how many dollars per month less it costs compared to what they're paying now to the utility. While it's a discussion point, it is not compelling to propose financing a $50,000 system so that a family can save $50-$100 per month. Generating enough money so they can go out to dinner at Applebee's once a month is not a top of mind issue for them. Energy independence and energy security is compelling and should be the focus of the conversation. Their financial well-being over the course of the next 30 years and whether or not they will be able to afford the electric bill for this home when they are retired is a good reason to say yes to a meeting. Now we're talking about avoiding disaster and winning the big ball game. That is compelling.

A common mistake that door-to-door sales people make at this point is to start selling the appointment. Don't do this. Appointments don't sound good. "How about I come back tomorrow night at about dinner time and do a presentation that will probably take 1 and 1/2 to 3 hours? Dinner will be late and of course you will miss *Survivor*. Does that sound good?" No. That does not sound good. The trick is to say a series of things that sound really good and then ask, "Does that sound good?"

I like to tell them what I'm going to do instead of asking them what they would like to do. I'll say, "Let's do this. I'm going to go back to my office and talk to my lead engineer. I'm going to have him pull up your roof on Google earth and see if it's awesome or terrible for solar. If it's terrible your home will not be suitable for the program and we won't need a meeting. If it's awesome then I'll have him complete the design, calculate the federal government investment and put together the complete 25 year profit projections. Then I'll come back when I have more time when you guys are free and will sit down and take a look at the numbers. I will be leaving you with a free design and numbers so that you can think about it. Does that sound good?"

Well guess what? That does sound good. They will often repeat those very words: "Yeah, that does sound good." Up to this point I have not mentioned anything about an appointment. Why? Because appointments with salesmen do not sound good. We've discussed that them getting the numbers to avoid disaster and accrue massive benefits does sound good.

Now the two of you have a mutual problem. You need to establish a time when you can come back when they are also free. This problem can be solved with a simple exercise of appointment setting.

"Thinking about your schedule, do you and Mrs. Johnson typically work during the day and are home around this time in the evenings or do one or both of you work from home these days? She works from home and you get home around 5 pm.? Now, tomorrow is Tuesday. Thinking about your calendar on Tuesdays, will tomorrow night work or would Wednesday evening be better? Wednesday is better? Excellent. Is 5:30 okay or would 6 pm be better?"

Stay with this process until a fixed day and time is agreed-upon. Ask one more time: "So Wednesday at 6 pm. Is there anything you can think of on Wednesday at 6 pm that would cause a problem?"

If the customer proposes that you call him first, push back with, "I'll be in several appointments throughout the day and will be heading straight over after the previous one. Here's my card with my cell phone number. If something happens and Wednesday at 6 pm and it isn't going to work, just text me and we can easily move it on the calendar."

You do not want to take on the task of calling them first because it will increase the likelihood of them canceling the appointment pretty significantly (for the same reason I do not call to confirm appointments). When they set the appointment, it's because getting the information sounds good. When you call on the day of the appointment and they think of all the things they have going on, sitting down with a salesperson for an hour or more does not sound good. You are better off doing your part and keeping the appointment and taking the risk that it may have to be rescheduled than to call in advance and increase the chances that it will. Yes, your time is valuable but there's no chance you will be wasting your time. If for some reason they're not able to make the appointment, then you have the perfect opportunity to knock on the neighbor's door with your tale of woe and why you're in the neighborhood. There's no chance that you're wasting your time. In fact, that's where the time to knock on doors comes from—being in the neighborhood.

If they are not moving forward with the appointment, I make them tell me no three times. I don't know why, but there's some kind of magic that happens between two and three. A lot of times it's because customers think it's their job to say no. And it is their job. How many offers come to a consumer on a daily basis? Television commercials, Facebook ads, telephone solicitations etc., and they have learned that they just have to say no. Everybody's got one no; most people have two no's. A lot of people don't have a third no. But if they have a third no in them, I'm going to get it out of them.

Oftentimes they will bring up an objection. "We are going to move someday. I don't like the way solar panels look on the house. We are going to need a new roof in a couple of years and we will be taking a look at solar after that."

There is an entire chapter on overcoming objections ahead. The basic framework at the door is to address the objection followed by a soft closing question such as, "does that make sense?" Then, come back with major benefits, bring up another urgency point, and then assert once again that you'll be having an engineer take a look at the roof. "He won't need to come out for that because we can see the roof from the satellite image on Google earth." Then come back with another closing question such as, "if the numbers show you making money immediately and demonstrate a profit of tens of thousands of dollars, I imagine you would want to see the numbers, am I right about that?" You may also try an inverted closing question such as, "If the numbers aren't terrific then you're not going to be interested, right?" This gives him the opportunity to say no which means yes to seeing the numbers.

Then I start asking for the routine information. "What is the correct spelling of your last name? I have your street address here, what is your ZIP Code? Does your home have one air conditioner or two? Do you have a pool? Is it heated? Do you currently have an electric vehicle? Are you planning to get one?" These questions are designed to get them thinking about their electric needs and to move the process forward to the appointment setting stage.

You can often ask a question that has the prospect saying her favorite word—no—which means she is saying yes to your proposition. "There's no way I could schedule an appointment without speaking with my husband first." To it you could respond, "Are you saying that he would be angry if you had an engineer provide you both with a free design?" "No, I don't think he would be angry…"

This is one of the more difficult objections to overcome: one spouse saying they need to speak with the other before setting the appointment. This is very often a brush off and can be addressed like any other objection—agree, new information, then ask for a new decision. "Of course you need to speak with your husband, in fact we would need you to both be at the appointment. I'll tell you what, you speak with your husband and I will speak with my engineer. If your roof is awesome for solar I'll have him put the design together and I'll come back when you and he have some time. By the way, my company appreciates your time and will be bringing a gift card for dinner to show our appreciation. Does your husband like Olive Garden or Outback steakhouse better? And what's the best email address to send the gift card to?" Now tell me that doesn't sound good?

If I have managed to generate some sincere interest but cannot get the homeowner to agree to an appointment on the spot, I will close for more information and an agreement to talk again soon. I will say "I'll tell you what, let me email you some information about the system. What's the best email address to send that to? Terrific. And what's the best cell phone number to follow up with you?" I mark this on my canvassing map with a green pin which are my strong lead call backs (SLCB). I regularly have SLCB sessions with my team. We will take turns calling one of these and revisiting the conversation. We very rarely do not set an appointment or two from the sessions. Also, any time I am in a neighborhood and looking for a no that I can turn into a yes, I will short for all of the green pins in the neighborhood and hit them first.

I'm going to make them tell me no three times. When they tell me no the third time, they are going to see the back of my head. Why? Because I'm off to the next door. I'm looking for the Easter egg.

I take the no and make it into a very pleasant experience—not for me but for them. I already know that I just made $100 to $500 for getting a no. I'm going to thank them with some real sincerity.

I'm going to tell them, "You know what's really tough about this? When folks don't take one minute to talk to us. This is a really tough job, and all we are trying to do is get the word out. You took a few minutes to talk to me, and I really appreciate it. That makes my whole day a lot better. I'm glad you got my business card. If you guys change your mind about getting the numbers, you let me know and I'll get the design done. Well, like I said, I've got to go." And with that, I'm on to the next door.

The reason we are on the street is to find the Easter egg. It makes no difference to me which one of these guys said yes, which one of these guys said no. It makes no difference to me if they were rude. It only makes a difference to me that one or more of these people said yes. I only care that I can look back and see that I have one or more purple Easter eggs.

Part 4

The Compelling Presentation

Chapter 11
Make a Friend, Make a Sale

When I walk into a house, my first job is to make a friend. I love being in other people's homes. I love being in someone's kitchen. If you are on Zoom, it's a lot harder, but you can still do it. That is: make a friend, make a sale. People like to do business with people they are friends with. Is it possible for you to become this person's friend, while only having five or ten minutes to do so?

It's not easy, but some people do have a knack for it. My partner Troy is great at it. He's one of those guys who you meet and immediately like. He's just got that likable personality. He's funny, and he thinks you're funny. And he's got this natural ability: every time he meets someone, within the first two or three minutes, he's made a buddy. Be thinking about that. If that's not your knack and you don't do it naturally, figure out ways to do it. That's what I'm pretty good at. I'm a natural-born sales guy; I'm kind of an outgoing, extroverted personality. But I'm more intellectual, so I have to think about how to do it.

The first thing you want to do when you walk into somebody's house is start looking at their trophies. Do they have bowling trophies, fishing trophies? Do they have pictures of their grandkids on the wall? Pictures of their kids' graduations on the wall? Do they have pictures of Hawaii or some kind of craft that they made? When you walk into someone's home, you are in their crib. Immediately, you can start taking inventory of what's important to them, what's of value to them. You want to take that inventory, grab one or two things, and then ask the customer about them. The most important thing about making a friend is not talking. The most important thing about making a friend is listening.

The key is to ask a specific question designed to tell you something important about them and then to follow that up with an open-ended question that gives them lots of room to tell you things about them that they enjoy talking about.

You can ask: "What do you do for a living? What business are you in?" Follow up with: "Wow, I've always been interested in engineering. How did you know you wanted to be an electrical engineer? Where did you go to school, and how did you go about picking the University of Michigan?" This last question will also shed light on their decision-making/purchasing process and values. You can ask: "What have you liked most about being a child psychologist?" or "What is the hard part about being a financial planner?"

You are trying to find an aspect of their life that provides significant self-esteem and get them talking about their wheelhouse. It will reveal much about their values, and it will give you some insight into what their ego is like and what it is about. When someone gets to expound on the subject that makes them valuable to their company, industry, family, and community, it brings them onto confident ground. It allows them to pass the baton to you to run onto your field of expertise from a place of mutual respect and affection. It enables them to accept your knowledge and wisdom as an exchange of value. If you can get them to tap into their passion and enthusiasm about their realm, it can often generate momentum that will carry over into your realm.

Before getting into solar sales, I sold IT networks to engineers for almost my entire adult life in my business-to-business (B2B) career, so I was always calling on very technical, geeky people. It's hard to get bonded with those people. The easiest way to do it was to ask them about a subject that they knew more about than anybody else on the planet. Engineers, technical people, the ones who are good with numbers: they are good with something they know more about than anyone else on the planet, and nobody wants to hear about it, including their spouse.

For example, if someone happens to be the plastics engineer of this, that, and the other, nobody wants to know about it. Be the person that really wants to know about it. And here's the trick to appearing interested in their area of expertise: actually *want* to know about it. If somebody is really your friend, you actually have affection for them. If somebody is a very good friend, you actually love them. If you can get to the point where you like the person you're sitting with, where you are getting them to tell you things that are endearing and cool about them, then you're actually going to like them—perhaps even love them.

That happens to me all the time. I end up meeting people, and by the time our interaction is over, we are hugging. I say, "It's genuinely so good to meet you," and it's not some salesy thing. I wouldn't go in for a hug with somebody if it was just some professional meeting and I just sold to them. Often, by the time I'm done with a meeting, I know these people and they know me. I told them a little bit about my family, and I've had them tell me quite a bit about their family. That's the easiest way to bond with someone. You want to ask about their kids: do any of their kids have some kind of special issue that they've dealt with? Is one of them a volleyball champion? What is their thing? Get that out of them and listen. I don't mean to sort of listen. I don't mean look at your phone while listening. I'm saying stop what you're doing, ask an open-ended question, and then put your elbows on the table, lean forward, and listen. Get good at what's called active listening. How in the world did your daughter get good enough at volleyball to win a scholarship to such a great school? Chances are the answer to that question is many hours of dedicated support from them over years, and they would love to talk about it but don't want to bore anybody about what a great parent they are to their kid. But be interested, be curious. Ask follow-up questions when you find that one thing and then *listen!*

Ask them where they like to go on vacation. Specific question: "What is it about Cabo San Lucas that makes you go back there?" Open-ended question: "Where are you folks from originally? What do you miss about Wisconsin? What made you choose Phoenix, Arizona, for your new home?"

Listen Intently Ask Open Ended Questions

- What do you like about living in California?
- How did you two meet?
- How did you discover you wanted to work in Education?
- What did it take to become a Project Manager in Construction?

Bill Clinton was tremendously popular as a president and as a person because he could make people understand that he could feel their pain. Anyone who would talk to him for a period of time would come away thinking, *He really gets me; he feels my pain.* And he would say to people: "I feel your pain." That man was one of the greatest salesman on planet Earth. If he could have met every single person in the United States, then he could have gotten every single person in the United States to vote for him. Once you met him, he would block out everything else that was going on around him. He would lean in and actually listen to you, and you would leave thinking, "That man really gets me. I want to support him."

That's the impact you want to achieve with your customer early on in the appointment. It may feel as though you are wasting valuable time that you could be using to spew important information about your project, but trust me: if you make time to become a true friend, meaning that you actually like and trust each other, they will then make time to do business with that friend. People like to do business with people they like. Plus, if they like you, they're going to want you to be happy by the end of this. Some of my longest appointments had a 20-minute presentation and close after an hour and a half of sincere, enthralling, life-enhancing conversation.

Make a friend: that's job number one.

Another valuable technique is to seek common interests and ways you can help each other. Knowing you could be really beneficial for them. I'm going to try to find those areas of common interest. "Oh, wow! No kidding. You're in the ABC business? My best friend happens to be vice president of manufacturing for the XYZ company. No kidding. I might be someone who could be a hookup for you. You guys like to go to Rocky Point, Mexico? My brother owns a place down there that he rents out to friends and family super cheap!"

Discover Common Interests

* Keep items about yourself brief "My brother is an Electrical Engineer
* Find ways your influence can benefit them "I have hundreds of customers and one of them is always needing ____ "

Now we've got a common interest, and they're going to start looking at me as someone whom they potentially want in their orbit and maybe even as an actual friend. I've got customers in my life who are friends because we do business. I make it a point to go out of my way to help those friends with their interests. This is not a casual thing or some salesman head fake. If you truly become friends, you will want to help them, and they will want to help you. If you want to see someone become a loyal customer and a wellspring of referrals, help them make a connection that boosts their own business or career.

I met my good friend Kelly Wu, the owner of Kawaii Sushi and Asian Cuisine by knocking on her door. We set an appointment, and she mentioned her three restaurants. I looked up her website and social-media pages before the appointment. We spent well over an hour talking about her business, how it started, all the family members she has working in it, the local marketing tools that we both use, and on and on. By the time we started talking solar, we were actual friends who had traded useful contacts, and writing up solar took 20 minutes.

I left her house with an appointment that she had made over the phone with her aunt and uncle, who speak very little English. She joined me for the meeting the next night. I just smiled and pointed at the design and numbers in the proposal as she sold them solar in Chinese. Since then, we have promoted each other's business in countless ways. I spend thousands of dollars a year buying restaurant gift cards to give to prospects as an enticement to sit for a presentation. I now buy gift cards from Kawaii and relish telling her neighbors in Peoria, Arizona, that they are going to have dinner at a restaurant owned by a neighbor of theirs and a friend of mine. We make a big deal about it on Facebook, and our circle of friendship grows and grows.

No matter where this endeavor to make a real friend goes, I always like to bring it back to homeownership. "How did you end up owning this home? Where did you move from to end up living at this home? What brought you from Indiana to California? What did you like about living in Indiana? How have you found California since you moved here?" Get them to talk. Be passionate about what excites them, and then you're going to be able to use that passion to generate the most valuable commodity in sales: enthusiasm. It's hard to fake enthusiasm. You may feel it about your product, but will they? If you can transfer genuine enthusiasm about what they are already truly passionate about into the conversation about solar, you are three quarters of the way home.

Bring it Back with their Home Ownership

- How long have you owned this home?
- Did you own you previous home?
- Who's idea was it to purchase instead of rent?
- The benefits of home ownership are the same as owning you own power plant

Then I ask a magical question: "OK, be honest: whose idea was it for you two to stop renting and to go look for a house to own?" Usually one will look at the other, and that one will get a big or sheepish smile and they will tell you the story: "We had been renting since before we were married, and he was buried with his new promotion at work. I called this realtor friend of mine...." This answer is magical because it will tell you so much about this couple and how they make purchasing decisions. It may give you specific insight as to who takes the lead in a big decision and who drags their feet. This will become very valuable information later. Most importantly, it will give you an opportunity to highlight benefits that have come from that action. Compliment them on their decision to become owners instead of renters. Much of your presentation will be to validate and attach the same benefits to their ability to make that kind of decision. This is especially true in solar. The benefits of homeownership and of power-plant ownership are almost identical. By utilizing their housing budget to pay down a mortgage instead of renting a home, they realize appreciation, equity, massive tax benefits, have a dramatic weapon against inflation, build wealth with money they were going to spend anyway, and, most importantly, benefit from a compounding return over many years.

As with owning a home, they are going to use "other people's money" to acquire an asset that will be paid for with money they were going to spend anyway, only significantly less each month instead of more in this case. It will increase the value of their home and add to their appreciation. Because the government is contributing a 26-percent subsidy to the project, they will immediately realize significant equity, which will increase over time as the payment reduces their balance to zero. The similarities are profound and immediately grasped by the homeowner when they see them side-by-side.

Your Friend in the Business is with the Right Company

When I start to present, I do it in an interstitial way. I'm not going to break out slides. "Interstitial" means I'm going to drop the facts about my company at an in-between moment. It might be when I'm walking through the door, or it might be just as we're sitting down. I'll bring up a fact, such as how we have 8,000 customers. I'm going to spend almost no time building a whole bunch of credibility for my company. I'm going to find a way, in an interstitial space, to drop facts about my company as if they're just facts—because they are facts.

One of the first things I'm going to do is make that customer feel confident that they have the right company at their house—that this is the way to go. All they're looking for is a check mark. They don't want to know your history; they don't want to know your problems; they don't want to know a bunch about you. They just want to know that they have the right person from the right solar company in their house. And why, ultimately, do they feel assured of that? Because we've been in business that long; we started in such and such year; we have 8,000 customers; we're rated 4.7 stars out of 5 on Facebook, etc. I like to make a joke about that: "Somehow we've managed to install this system for 8,000 families, and not a single person wants to kill us." I'll talk about a handful of things in an "Oh, by the way" fashion just to get them the check mark, and then I'll move on.

We've got a lot of ground to cover with a customer. I'm not going to spend 15 minutes giving them my company's credentials. I'm going to spend a minute and a half, getting them to think, *OK, check mark. Right company.* They want to feel confident that they have conscientious, established, experienced people—and that these people have decent pricing, as evidenced by the fact that a lot of people are buying their product.

Chapter 12
Build the Door Frame

You want your prospects to understand that you have a job to do and that that job as owner/consultant/advisor is to meet with them today. We are going to make sure the design is right, educate them on the elements that make this solution so powerful, and help them get all of their questions answered so that we can figure out if this solution is going to be fantastically beneficial for them. I let them know that I meet with three or four families every day to accomplish this, and if they're not sure it makes sense for them or they need more time, I have a world-class sales department that will stay in touch with them and will get them any additional information they need to make a terrific decision for themselves and their family. In fact, everything I am going to cover will have details and prices in the proposal, which I will leave here with you. That pricing will be good for 30 days. My message is: "Relax, friends. I will get you everything you are hoping to get out of the meeting, and you will have all the time in the world to make a great decision for your family. *No pressure.*"

Building the Frame

- Have a Plan
- Explain Plan and Set Expectations
- "It's my job to......"
  - Educate you to the point where you can say yes or no to moving forward with solar today
  - I meet with 3 or 4 brand new customers every day. If this is making tons of sense then then part of my job is to help you get the process started today
  - If not...that OK we want your business. I will be emailing your free design which is good for 30 days and I will have our sales department follow up with you.
- Fair enough, lets get started!

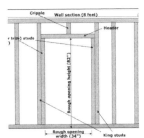

I like to think of two metaphors when I start my presentation.

The first metaphor is that I'm a lawyer. I'm going to be speaking to the ladies and gentlemen of the jury, and I'm going to be presenting evidence to them, at the conclusion of which I'll be asking them to reach a verdict. I'm going to guide them along a logical path, at the end of which they really have no decision but to sign up and go solar today.

"Ladies and gentlemen of the jury, my job is to make sure we've got the right design on the house, to make sure that you understand how solar works, to make sure you understand the process, and, if this is making a ton of sense to you, to get the process started today. Sound good?" (I always start out by telling people what my job is, which specifically does not include coming back.)

"Now, if this doesn't make sense for you, that's okay. We've got a sales force, and these people are really good at following up. That's not my job—I'm not on the comeback team. My job, as a consultant/owner/trainer, is to be in three or four homes with brand-new customers every single day—that's my job. It's somebody else's job to come back if you don't want to buy today, which is perfectly all right. We want your business, and we will be ready when you're ready. Does that make sense? Let's get started."

What is this conversation designed to tell them? I'm telling them several things, actually. I am an owner of the company, so I play the owner card. If you are a consultant or energy advisor, then play that card and tell them what the job entails. But the moral of the story is to help them understand that you are not the comeback person. Your company has people for that. It's called the sales department. Your message is very clear: if this is making sense to them and they are decisive people, then we are going to get the process started. I'm going to be walking this project into my company's installation department because they have "engaged" a contractor to begin working for them. We're going to be getting this onto the schedule and start defeating our common enemy, which is time. If they're not ready, then we're going to be leaving them with a free design proposal that will have most of the information we discuss in this meeting, and I'll be turning over this project to our sales department, where they have effectively become a lead. This frame lets them know that I will not be coming back, not because I am a jerk but because I have a job to do, and it doesn't include hounding them forever until they're ready to make a decision. We have very good professional salespeople who will be following up with them, and our company will be ready when they are ready. Again, no pressure. Later on, when they're telling me they just need a few days and can I come back, I'm going to remind them about what my job is and isn't. I'm also going to explain to them that if we move forward today, my company has one set of costs. If we employ this other department to follow up with them at a later date, the company will have additional costs to deal with. Then I'm going to show them how we're going to turn that fact to their benefit.

"Let me tell you, we've got the best follow-up salespeople on the planet. These guys are good at what they do. Don't worry that you'll forget about solar because they're going to make sure you never forget about solar. They're going to be in your ear three times a week trying to figure out when you're ready to go solar, and that'll be great for me because I'm the owner and I hope you go solar someday. However, if you've seen enough to get started, It's my job to get the project started, and we will kick it off right away."

The other metaphor that I like to think of is that I am building a door frame. "It's my job to come to your home and get the process started and then make sure I've understood what your objectives are, make sure that our design meets the criteria of those objectives, show you the design, and answer all of your questions. And then it's my job to get the process started. If you've heard enough to make a decision, we will get the paperwork done. I will take your design into the office, get the installation department started the very next morning and get them introduced to you and all of those sorts of things. And that's my job. Now, if that's not enough, and you haven't seen enough to make a decision, that's fine, too. We do want your business. In fact, the proposal I've brought will show you that the price is good for 30 days. So this is not a high pressure operation. I'm going to leave you with a free proposal. I'm also going to buy you dinner just for having me over. We appreciate people taking time to review our company to consider our solution, our company, and our qualifications. Do you like Olive Garden or Cheesecake Factory better? Cheesecake Factory? Me too. My wife loves Cheesecake Factory. We're buying you dinner just for having us over, no matter what. I've got a free estimate for you. It's good for 30 days and there's no pressure whatsoever. However, my job is to meet with you, do the things that I just said, and then to help you get the process started, if you've seen enough to make a decision. If you're not, no problem. I'm also in charge of the sales department. And I have literally 25 guys who work for me and I'll be assigning one of them to just follow up with you and get the information that you need over time. And when you're ready, we'll be there for you. Fair enough. Does that sound like a plan? Yes? Ok, then let's get started."

Even if they like your product and they like you, they're going to want you to get back. Which is why I can't emphasize enough to not fall for those traps and to let them know you are not coming back under any circumstances.

The other thing is it's going to sound a lot better being one of the owner's or consultant's customers than the customer of some salesman.

And by the way, every single sales person in America as a 1099 salesperson is the owner. They're the owner of their small business. They will feel better knowing they have you to be personally in charge of getting their project off the ground. All with no pressure.

They decide: Are we going to fish or are we going to cut bait? You want to fish? I got the boat out back. It's all loaded up with beer fishing poles. I got sandwiches. We're gonna have a great time. You want to cut bait? Bye. I'll put you on the list of people who are out cutting bait.

Which one of those sounds better to you? They're going to decide to go fishing. You're asking them to make a decision either way. Do you want to go on an awesome fishing outing? Or do you want to stay on the shore and cut bait? If you'd like to go fishing, step aboard. No one's going to want to be left on the shore.

When you build something, you have a plan. I'm going to explain the plan to the person. "I'm the guy who meets with three, four people a day and helps them understand everything. They're running me ragged. Now that we have a Green New Deal and everybody's going solar, they're literally having me working Sundays. I'd love to come back, but I'm not going to be able to come back because I'm not that guy and I don't have the time to do that." Why? Because I meet with three or four brand-new customers every day. What I'm doing is building a frame, and I'm going to drive them through that frame as if it were a corral.

"I'm here, you're here, and if we are going to do this business together personally, we're going to have to get the process started today. That doesn't mean we can't give you all the time in the world for you to validate your decision to move forward with solar. But if you want to do business with me and take advantage of the opportunity that's available today, then we're going to have to get the process started today. If you're not ready, that is perfectly fine. I will be leaving (and not coming back) with a proposal that is good for 30 days, and we will be ready when you are."

Now, remember: my job is to get the no. If I am in 10 solar presentations per week, and seven customers move forward while three say no to signing today, am I even the least bummed out? Maybe for a minute. But in reality, one week from now I won't remember their name, let alone care whether they were one of the three no's. Now, if they make a decision and move forward, then we really are going to be friends. We are going to be in each other's lives. My company will be making sure this system delivers their power needs for 25 years.

As Coach Micheal Burt likes to tell customers: "I cannot help you if you won't commit. But once you do make a commitment, I will not let you fail."

You want to be a no? You want to become a sales lead? I'm not even going to complain about it.

In the presentation we are going to actually hang the door in this frame. What are we going to do with this door that we have hung in this frame? Close it.

Serving the customer at the highest level means more than just educating them on the product; it also means showing them the benefits. And that's how you transition.

Do you see the benefits?

It feels like this is making a lot of sense for you. Am I right about that?

It seems like a perfect fit for you guys. Are you ready to take the next step?

I could craft those three sentences a hundred different ways. The important thing is that you craft a sentence that feels good coming out of your mouth and you're asking them to buy. If they step aboard, get the paperwork going. But if they don't step aboard, now it's time to go to work. Now it's time to actually go to work and be the reason that they sent me instead of a YouTube video.

Again, it doesn't matter what the story is, but the story needs to be genuine and, hopefully, heartwarming. And it needs to make a point that you're not coming back.

This part of the conversation for me:
- Because solar energy is abundant and free, your family will receive tremendous financial benefits and peace of mind;
- You will get away from destructive carbon-based energy, which means you will avoid the consequences of its demise;
- We have put a check mark next to going solar and provisioning your power for decades.

Now relax and let my company take care of everything.

Chapter 13
Hang the Door—From Education to Understanding to Knowledge

We built that frame, and we're preparing to guide the customer through that frame and into a dead end where they have no choice but to make a decision today. The body of the presentation is where we hang the door. There is a tremendous amount of information that we could choose from to present to the customer. However, there is not enough time, and it is not necessary for them to know everything that you know about your product. There is no way they can know everything anyway. Nonetheless, there are elements that are essential for the customer to know so they can understand the benefits and, even more important, the pitfalls of not having the product. We want them to go through this process and end up with knowledge. When people invest time to learn about a solution to a dire problem, they end up having knowledge that most people do not have, and they experience an urgent need to use that knowledge to their benefit.

You're not pitching; you're educating. What I do is actually put on a little class, and in that little class, I'm about to show the customer what the insiders know. When it comes to solar, I am the best teacher. I talk to them about the solar systems out there, the fact that solar is a big industry and that there are things about it that they don't know. And what I'm about to do is impart knowledge to them—not information. I'm not going to tell them the specs about a solar panel and give them all sorts of crazy scientific information. I'm not going to lecture them about the environment. I'm going to impart knowledge, not information. I'm going to show them what the smart people know and make them an insider.

Build then Hang the Door

- Utility Company
- Tax Credits
- Inflation and a the Green New Deal
- Design - Production and Equipment
- Warranties and Monitoring
- The Money - If we can make the money make sense, is there any reason it wouldn't make sense to go solar?!

My presentation is the beginning of a process of educating them and getting them to understand what's going on, why people buy this, and what problems they're going to have if they don't buy it. For example, even if they don't go solar, they're going to have knowledge about two or three things that are going to help them save money because I'm going to explain how their utility company makes money.

And one of the things that makes me good at what I do is my ability to efficiently learn technical information and present it accessibly and compellingly. If you dropped me into any company anywhere in the world, I could spend a day or two or three hearing the technical people tell me what their product is and why it's awesome, and then I could explain it to a new customer better than anybody who works for that company. The reason why I could explain it so well is because I'm going to talk about three big things in a presentation. It will depend on the product or service, but you need to identify three areas of knowledge they need to know.

Tell them, "The first thing you need to know is A," and then wrap that up.

"The second thing you need to know is B." Then go through that and wrap it up. "Is there anything more I can tell you about that?"

"And the third thing you need to know about is C."

I'm going to spend time on each of those three things since most of my time with a customer will be spent educating them. Why? Because if they have that knowledge, they understand it, and they feel like they have a command of it, then they're going to have the confidence to make a decision.

And I'm going to do that with passion and enthusiasm. That's the key. My passion and enthusiasm are going to propel knowledge from my mind to theirs, thereby creating the conviction they need to make a decision. *Step on the boat. The boat is leaving.* If I'm going to be successful in convincing them to step on the boat, then they will need to have confidence and be excited about the boat. And I'm going to build that excitement by giving them the knowledge, the insider's view. I'm going to have them understand what the smart people know and what the ignorant people don't know. The smart people on the street have solar whereas the ignorant people on the street don't have solar because they're ignorant. That's not an insult—that's a state of being. If someone doesn't know the reasons why a person would make the decision to do this, that's ignorance. I'm going to cure the ignorance; I'm really going to have them understand why this is happening and how it works. And they're going to go from ignorant to knowledgeable. Because knowledge makes people money.

When it comes to solar, for example, I'm first going to explain the electric utility. Then I'm going to explain how the government is incentivizing solar and what's going to happen if they take that incentive—and what's going to happen if they don't take that incentive. I'm going to break down that incentive, how it works, and how it turns into $25,000 in cash in their hands. I'm going to show them how that works and take all the mystery out of it. And I'm going to lead them to see that they've just been ignorant about it until now. Now that they've gone from ignorance to knowledge with respect to how the utility and the tax credits work, it would now be an act of stupidity not to move forward, and I'm going to tell them that.

In the process of explaining how the tax credit works, I will show them little graphs and draw it all out for them. I say the government is providing the tax credit to achieve two goals. One is to give them the financial incentive to make this investment. The other is to literally make the alternative look stupid. I'm going to show them a graph that illustrates where they will end up if they stay with the utility: spending hundreds of thousands of dollars more than if they pull the trigger on solar. Furthermore, I show how they could end up in a precarious situation, one in which they experience some financial distress and might even need to sell their home because they did not pull the trigger back in 2022. In 10 years, they could end up in a situation where they've made a fatal mistake, but now that they're educated, that doesn't have to become reality. If they don't pull the trigger now that they're knowledgeable, it's on account of stupidity rather than ignorance.

What I'm primarily explaining to people is that, although the cost of electricity has been doubling every 15 years for the last 60 years, it's not just going to double in the next 15 years. It's gone from two and a half cents to a nickel to 10 cents to 20 cents. But it's not going from 20 cents to 40 cents, and that's because the government has decided that fossil fuels are done. We don't know if that's 10 years from now, 20 years from now, or 30 years from now, but fossil fuels are done. And they're offering incentives. That's the carrot.

I say: "I'm going to show you how the tax credits work. That's a huge, $20,000 carrot. If you don't take the carrot, you're going to get the stick. Before now, you were ignorant about the carrot, and now that you understand it, I'm going to let you know that the stick is coming. And if you don't commit, you could literally end up not being able to afford to stay in your house anymore."

What I'm showing them is leading them to the conclusion that it would be stupid not to buy. That's the key.

When you're educating, it's important to highlight concepts, not features. I'm not going to tell them anything about the features of a solar system. I'm going to explain to them why it's smart to get the system and stupid not to. I'm going to give them the knowledge that turns the benefits into something they can see and touch. I'm not going to show them PowerPoint slides—I draw it on graph paper. And then I'm going to have them walk this journey with me. If they stay with the plan they're on now, the cost will increase exponentially, and they're going to end up in trouble.

I have them really grasp that by imagining it. I ask them: "Can you imagine living in this home, and your electric bill hasn't doubled, but rather tripled? And now instead of $4,000 a year, you're paying $12,000 a year for heating and cooling? Can you imagine, 10 years from now, having done A, B, or C and no longer encountering X, Y, or Z?"

And I show them the graph. "Would you rather end up here when you're retired 15, 20, 25 years from now, or would you rather end up here? Which is it?"

Take them on that journey. Walk them down the path of having said yes and the path of having said no.

You might be wondering how long this should take. There's no right answer. I closed a 28-kilowatt sale on Thursday and a 30-kilowatt deal on Friday. Those are monstrously large solar systems, and I was in the house three hours on one and almost five hours on the other. How do I explain the difference in duration? Let's say you invite me to come to your house and take your grandmother for a walk around the block, and you ask me, "How long is it going to take to accompany so-and-so's grandmother on a walk around the block?" Well, I would have no idea; It's different for everybody. But I could make an estimate at some point during the walk according to my perception of some relevant factors. How fast is she walking? Does she need to stop and take breaks? Or is she the spry little sprinter of a grandma, and I'm going to have to keep up with her? I'm not going to know that till I'm on the walk.

It's the timeline between walking in their front door, when they're ignorant and undecided, and finally making them knowledgeable enough to make a decision, and it's just like the timeline of taking your grandmother for a walk around the block. I have zero idea how long it will take right now, but once I'm on the walk, I'll be able to tell.

So if I have another appointment that starts in two hours, and I'm starting to put them on my clock, or for whatever reason, my presentation takes a set amount of time, no matter what I do, I'm going to end up doing it at my speed. But if I do it at their speed, I'm going to take the time to make sure they're with me, and if they're not with me, I'm going to pause, back up a little bit, and start again. I'm going to make sure they're with me every step of the way.

Let's come back to my three things. When it comes to solar, I'm going to explain to them the electric utility and how their interaction with that entity works. The second thing I'm going to do is explain to them how the government is subsidizing solar and wanting them to go solar. Those are the tax credits. And the third thing I'm going to do is explain what's going to happen to them if they don't go solar, which is all about inflation. And I'm going to have a story for each one of those topics. In my presentation, I'm going to deliver on that.

Most salespeople actually think, *If I explained it to the customer, then they definitely got it.* But I can't tell you how many times I've explained all the aspects of solar to someone and the husband's on board but not the wife. That's when I ask, "Mary, if the solar was on the roof right now and making power, what would you be concerned about?"

And you might hear, "Well, I'm just worried that if I use more power on air conditioning, the freezer's going to go off, and I'm going to lose all the food in my freezer."

And I'm thinking, *Holy cow, how in the world could she have listened to my presentation and ended up worried that if they use more power, then the solar system will make their freezer shut off?* So never assume that because you explained it, they got it. In fact, they are probably only picking up maybe 15, 20, or 30 percent. In the process of your sale, especially if you're doing a solar sale, you are not going to teach them everything in your head. I've tried before. What you are actually trying to do is transfer the confidence and the conviction that you have so that they believe they don't need to understand everything there is to know. As long as they know that I know everything there is to know and I am convinced they are way better off, then we're good.

Chapter 14
The Advanced Solar Presentation—The Four Big Things

If you work in solar sales, this chapter is for you. But even if you don't, you can still learn a thing or two, so don't skip it because what I do every day is meet people at their home and talk about home improvement, and there's a lot to be learned from this massive category. When you walk in the door, that's the beginning of an hour-and-a-half to two-and-a-half-hour process of getting them to sign a five-figure contract. That journey starts with them opening the door and you establishing a connection—or, as we've talked about in this book, making a friend and combating their fear.

The heart of the solar presentation is going to be about four subjects that have nothing to do with solar panels and everything to do with the benefits of going solar. Those four subjects are:

1. Tax credits and incentives
2. Utility export-credit policies
3. Inflation and the Green New Deal
4. Ownership

Tax Credits

I like to start out with the tax credits because I want to explore the prospect's individual tax situation. Specifically, I want to determine whether they have a tax liability with which to take advantage of the tax credit.

All families will typically receive a tax credit of somewhere between $7,000 and $25,000. This is very often explained to the customer in a way that leads them to believe that it is a rebate or a grant from the federal government, but it is not. It is crucial that this be explained very clearly so they know exactly how they will receive that subsidy. If their personal finances and income are such that they do not generate much or any tax liability, then they will receive the credit but won't have anything to apply it against and will not end up receiving the funds in a timely manner. If they have a tax credit but no liability, the credit will carry forward to future years until they do have a liability, but it will not produce an immediate benefit.

If this is the case, you will want to make sure to propose a power purchase agreement (PPA) or a lease. In these financing vehicles, the finance company or leasing company takes advantage of the tax credit and works that benefit into the monthly payment. And that way, a low income family or individual with a very low tax liability can still receive the benefit of the solar ITC.

I want to make sure I have the right proposal. I either brought the proposal with me or one of my engineers is finishing it up while I'm there. I want to make sure that I am showing them the solution that is right for them. The last thing in the world I want to do is show them two or three proposals and then have them wondering, *Which way should I go?* Then they have an actual and legitimate objection, which is that they don't know which solution to go with. So you have to understand what solution is best for them, and that is dictated by their tax situation.

I generally prefer showing purchases. But if somebody doesn't have the income to take advantage of the tax credits, then I want to make sure I switch out my proposal to a leasing or PPA arrangement before actually proposing it. So the first thing I want to cover with them is the information I need to determine the best solution for them. And to do that, I need to make sure that the tax credits are clearly explained and that they are confident they will be able to use them.

I usually peek ahead to the proposal to see the size of the tax credit. Let's say the design generates a $12,000 tax credit. I explain that this amount is going to be subtracted from the bottom line of their tax return, which spells out their total liability. If that money has been withheld from their paychecks all year, they're going to receive a refund in the amount of that tax credit, which in this case is $12,000, as long as their liability and withholdings are more than that figure. In the event that their liabilities and withholdings are less than $12,000, the IRS will zero out their total liability and refund any withholdings. So if their tax credit is larger than their current year's tax liability, the remaining amount will be carried forward to future years' tax liabilities. They will still get the full credit, but it may not be used in the first year. If this is the situation, it will need to be made clear to the homeowner that this could affect how much and when they apply this tax credit to their loan, which could affect the buydown amounts and projected monthly payment. Most solar financing loans anticipate that the customer will apply the tax-credit amount in month 18 or in month 36, so they will display an initial monthly payment and a future monthly payment based on that assumption. The proposal should also show what the future monthly payment will be if they do not apply that tax credit. If they will receive only a partial amount of the tax credit, they may have to add some of their own savings or anticipate a higher monthly payment to compensate.

Many states also have direct financial incentives for homeowners to apply to a solar purchase. For instance, Arizona offers a tax credit amounting to 25 percent of the purchase price, capped at $1,000 total, and this state tax credit works the same way as the federal version. As long as the purchaser has a tax liability of $1,000 or more, they will receive that as a cash benefit in the first year. If their tax liability is less, the credit will carry forward to the next year.

I typically don't get into the individual homeowner's specific finances, but on a piece of paper I explain the basics. It sounds somewhat complicated, but they all file taxes every year and typically grasp this very quickly. I explain that at the end of the year, they will receive a W-2 or 1099 form that shows them their income and how much money has been withheld from their paychecks. Then they will complete their 1040, which will tell them how much money the government is going to keep. In a typical year, if their withholdings are greater than their liability, then they will receive a cash refund. If their withholdings are less than their total tax liability, they will owe money and will have to send a check with their return. This leads to tremendous confusion over how much an individual or family pays in taxes. They typically remember this refund or payment amount and not the amount of the total tax liability. It is astounding how many people think that because they receive a refund they don't actually pay taxes. This will lead them to think that the tax credit associated with a solar purchase will not help them.

To describe how the tax credit works, I ask them to imagine that in the middle of the year and for no reason they send a check to the IRS for $12,000. Will the IRS employee look up their account, discover that they didn't owe any taxes, and send a check back? No, they will deposit the check, and it would show up as a credit on their IRS account. This credit would apply to how much money the government expected them to pay that year. This is exactly what the solar tax credit does for them, only without their having to send any money to the IRS. Essentially, the next $12,000 in federal taxes that the government would expect you to pay has already been paid and is sitting in your account as a credit.

It is important to explain that this is real money. Otherwise, people have a tendency to think it will get lost in the blizzard of pluses and minuses on their tax return. It can be particularly difficult to get a self-employed person or independent contractor (who files a Form 1099) to believe the credit will be realized in full. They often believe that, since they don't have any money withheld from their checks and therefore receive no refunds, that the credit is not real money. If they are doing their own quarterly withholdings, then they will receive a refund unless they adjust those quarterly payments to take into account the solar credit. But many 1099 contractors do not send in quarterly withholdings, so at the end of the year they have to write a check with a penalty applied for not doing the withholdings. And they will complain that they didn't get a refund. Of course they didn't get the refund; what they received instead stays in their account all year and represents the amount of money they will not have to send to the IRS. This is actually a more powerful benefit, but it may not seem that way because no one sent them any money.

You need to mentally seize on the idea of a credit and transfer into their head the fact that it's real money. I cannot tell you how many people I've talked to who tell me they don't pay taxes. Why would somebody tell me that they don't pay taxes if they are working and making good money? Because at the end of the year, they don't pay anything to the government; it was just taken directly out of each paycheck. When I explain this phenomenon to new customers, they laugh because they see how silly it is. But you will be surprised by how many people actually think that since they are getting money back, they actually don't pay taxes. Well, let me tell you, if you are alive and you are working, you are paying taxes.

I like to tell a little allegory about casinos. I explain that the person who invented gambling was smart, but the one who invented chips was a genius. Likewise, the government deciding to tax individuals' income was definitely a windfall, but the idea of withholding the tax from paychecks was a game changer. If Americans had to pay their full tax liability out of their bank account every spring, we would have the Boston Tea Party every year. This analogy helps them understand that their apparent lack of tax liability is just an illusion, and it thereby helps them see the value of the tax credit. I will say, "Mr. Customer, the refund is not you getting your taxes back. They are sending the overpayment back and keeping the taxes you owe. The tax credit is going to lower the amount they keep by $12,000, and that means they are going to add $12,000 to your refund."

I always talk to people about the tax credit as money coming to them that they can do anything they like with. "Put that towards the solar, and I'll show you what that does to the payment. Or you can take that $12,000 and go on a trip around the world. You can take that $12,000 and build a pool or put it directly into your retirement account. You can be $12,000 closer to retiring, and I'll show you what that does to the payment as well. You will have the option to do anything you like. It's your money."

It's important to be up to date on what the current tax credits are. As of this writing in 2022, the tax credit would have dropped from 22 percent to 0 percent if it had followed its previous schedule. After having been extended, it was scheduled to drop from 26 percent to 22 percent at the beginning of 2021, but Congress again extended it at the 26-percent rate for an additional two years via one of the Covid-19 relief bills, so the 2022 solar ITC is still 26 percent. Biden's Build Back Better bill has provisions to increase the tax credit to 30 percent and extend it an additional 10 years. It also has a provision to make the tax credit refundable, which would give low-income families the opportunity to go solar. In effect, they would receive the tax credit as a grant and could apply it to a solar purchase even though they don't have a tax liability. That bill is currently stalled, and the future of those provisions is uncertain. The current schedule has the tax credit decreasing from 26 percent to 22 percent on January 1, 2023, and then to zero on January 1, 2024. As a solar salesperson, you should be emphasizing this very short window that the customer has to go solar with the maximum tax credit, and you should be communicating the urgency that they take advantage of that and move forward today.

The customer's choice is to go solar with the current tax credits or to go solar after they are gone. They will almost certainly be going solar in the near future due to the ever-increasing cost of energy and the carbon-emission-reduction targets agreed to by the United States when it re-entered the Paris Climate Accord in January, 2021, which effectively set America on a path toward a Green New Deal. As this book is being edited, Russia has just invaded Ukraine, and the United States has banned the importation of Russian oil and gas to any United States ports. We are seeing a massive surge of energy prices, which will bring the question of green energy to the consumer much more abruptly then we have been anticipating. Homeowners have a very short window to take advantage of the tax credits and purchase solar before these massive energy-price increases ripple through to the cost of solar panels.

Utilities

When the homeowner installs solar, it will be connected to the grid. The credit system in effect between them and their electric company will dramatically affect the way their solar system produces savings. There will be periods when the solar system is underproducing and the customer is getting a portion of their electricity demand from the grid. There will be times (at night, for instance) when the system is producing nothing and they are getting all their power from the grid. There will be other times when the solar system is producing more power than the household needs and is exporting the surplus energy back to the grid. In this instance, the electric utility will credit the consumer for that power.

Explain to the customer that the meter on the side of their house is what they use to purchase power from the utility currently. When they install solar, there will be a second meter installed that will keep track of how much power they sell back to the utility company. In reality, most meters today are bidirectional, but there are usually two meters out there on account of the utility company or the leasing company tracking how much the system produces. In any case, I like to use the simplistic idea that they will have one meter for buying and one meter for selling. It is of paramount importance that you have a comprehensive understanding of how the credit system works with respect to metering and pricing.

In my notebook, I will draw the meter they have on their house now and explain how they're currently being charged for power. If they have the time-of-use system, they will have different prices for on-peak and off-peak periods. I will then draw a second meter and show how they're being compensated for any of the power they generate and export to the grid. Most utilities used to use, and some still do use, a net-metering system whereby the total energy produced by the solar system over a month was subtracted from the total energy received from the grid, yielding either a surplus or a deficit that would be credited or debited to the customer according to the standard price per kilowatt-hour. The benefit of this system is that it was one to one. The market I am in, Arizona, did away with net metering in 2017 and instead uses a cash-metering system. In Arizona, electric utilities purchase and sell units of energy for different prices, so the monthly bill reflects the difference between the total purchase and sale totals, irrespective of the relative value of the energy amounts themselves. At the end of the year, any remaining surplus is sent to the customer as a check.

There are many variations of this credit system. They vary from one utility to another in the same market. It is absolutely essential that you understand which utility your customer is connected to and how that credit system works, and you need to be able to explain that in detail so that the customer completely understands it. Your proposal needs to be completed by an engineering department that understands the math of this credit system and applies it to the production and usage. That way, the customer has an idea of how much money they will still owe the utility in addition to what they're paying for solar.

This is a source of a lot of confusion for homeowners and is one of the reasons they may have a negative view of solar. They have probably heard people in their neighborhood talk about going solar and still having a large utility bill. Understanding the dynamics of the credit system will enable you to recommend a design that accomplishes what the customer's objectives are. Markets that have net metering typically also have connection fees, and you want to be sure the customer understands what they will be charged by the utility company above and beyond what they pay for Solar.

Depending on the credit system, it may be beneficial for the customer to produce significantly more power than they consume in a year. If they're on a cash-metering system, this can be used to generate cash that will illuminate the utility company's connection charges. It also may make sense to design the system so that it makes enough power to include future electric-vehicle purchases or a new pool, with or without a pool heater.

In the Arizona market, we regularly sell customers a solar system that produces 140 percent of the power that they typically consume in a year. This additional power serves two purposes. If they end up needing more power for any reason, they already have it on board and don't need to expand the system. In the meantime, we sell those kilowatt-hours to the utility, and it generates surplus cash that wipes out most if not all of their remaining bill for connection charges, taxes, etc. If you design the system so that it generates 100 percent of the power the customer uses in a year, the remaining bill is more significant than many solar companies will tell them. By addressing the significant remaining amount on the bill and showing them a larger system that will eliminate it, you can demonstrate to the customer how more solar means a lower, not greater, cost of energy. Instead of paying $140 for a 100-percent system and still owing the utility $40 to $50 a month on average, the customer can get more panels and more power for $175 per month and end up paying a little less, not more, per month. "Mr. Customer, did you want 30 panels for 180 a month, or did you want 39 panels for 175 a month? It's five dollars a month less expensive to get 30 percent more panels and power."

You have to learn about your utility and understand how its particular credit scheme works. If the utility has net metering, it may cost 10 cents to make the additional power, whereas they could be getting only 3 cents back. Therefore, overproduction may not be beneficial in that case.

I cannot express how important it is to your long-term success to make sure you are understanding what the customer's total cost of electricity will be, including the remaining utility bill, and having that spelled out in writing in the proposal. It may seem like a good idea to leave that part out of the conversation and out of the proposal, but in the long run that will really bite you and your company in the backside. You will end up under siege from customers who are actually saving money but are terribly unhappy because their results are different from their expectations.

I'll tell you what I've learned after selling solar for as many years as I have. Almost every single person, after going solar, is going to want more solar. They are almost always going to want more power. Why? In addition to the electric vehicle that is certain to be in their future, as well as other appliances they may want or need, their attitude about electricity will go from a mindset of scarcity to one of abundance. They are going to go from stingy to relaxed. This will drive up their hunger for more power.

The grid was built for centralized power production and distribution. The introduction of solar systems into neighborhoods is an example of distributed power systems. The grid was not designed for this and has many challenges. As more and more solar systems are being installed, many local utilities are lobbying the regulatory bodies for changes to their credit system and limits to how many systems can be attached to the grid.

The changes that are coming to your local utility are one of the most powerful sources of the urgency that needs to be communicated to the customer. If net metering is still available in their area, they need to jump on it immediately because it will definitely be changing in the near future. If they have a cash-credit system, there are often scheduled dates at which the relevant numbers are set to change. The utility may have set up tranches defining how many consumers can sign up on a given plan before a new plan replaces it with numbers far less advantageous to the customer. Understanding this and communicating it to the customer gives you the opportunity to sell solar while a gun is pointed at the customer's head—and you are not the one holding the gun. This will create deadlines that you and the customer have no power over, and that generates urgency. They must act now to take advantage of the current system. In almost all cases, there will be a period of time during which a new customer is grandfathered into the old system, but they must act now!

The step-by-step process of reviewing the customer's utility bill and demonstrating the effect of the two meters can be found in the MOD Sales Academy at www.modsalesacademy.com.

Inflation

How much does solar cost? In almost all markets across the country, solar costs less than what the customer is already paying for electricity from their utility. How much less? It could be $30 a month; it could be $100 a month. This may or may not be a compelling reason to purchase, and in most instances will finance a $30,000 to $60,000 solar system for the particular homeowner you're presenting to. However, it is certainly not the most important reason why the customer should convert to solar ASAP. The primary issue that the customer is dealing with is one that they often don't perceive. Inflation is an insidious force and a relentless one. Over any period of time, all products and services become more expensive due to inflation.

When I was in grade school and Jimmy Carter was president, the nation was dealing with upwards of 7-percent inflation, 21-percent interest rates, and surging energy costs, which were a multiple of what they had been a few short years before. Ronald Reagan was elected in a landslide to change many things, but more than anything else to fix the economy and bring inflation to heel. Since that time, the nation has had inflation in the range of roughly 2 to 4 percent. I have been showing the financial benefits of solar for many years using 25-year electricity-cost projections that assume that historical rate of inflation. In my proposal, I clearly demonstrate that the cost of electricity will in fact double in the next 15 years. When I look at historical prices for kilowatt-hours, it has in fact doubled every 15 years since the 1960s, when electricity cost approximately 2 1/2 cents per kilowatt-hour. Those prices have reliably doubled approximately every 15 years to get us to the prices that we pay today. Eliminating the doubling of your electrical costs In the next 15 years is an extremely compelling reason to go solar. If you can avoid increasing your residential energy costs from $3,000 to $6,000 a year over the next 15 years and do it without spending more money (in fact, paying less every month for solar), it literally doesn't make any sense not to do this.

As I write this in March of 2022, the United States is dealing with $10 trillion of Covid-19 spending that was spent to make the pandemic shutdown seem like a vacation. The current inflation rate is reported to be approximately 7.9 percent. This is not Ronald Reagan-era inflation. This is Jimmy Carter-era inflation. Actually, if we used the same model to calculate the Consumer Price Index (CPI) that we used in the '70s, it is said that the current inflation rate would be reported as 15 percent.

In addition to this high inflation, the United States has re-entered the Paris Climate Accord and has committed to reducing its carbon emissions by 50 percent before the end of the decade. This reminds me of the famous "moon shot" that President Kennedy declared in 1961, committing the United States to put a man on the moon before the end of the decade. The country was incredulous that this could possibly be done; many were worried that we would bankrupt ourselves trying. Nevertheless, on June 20, 1969, Neil Armstrong stepped out of the lunar lander, making one small step for man and one giant leap for mankind. Likewise, some people do not believe we can possibly cut our emissions in half by 2030. However, when you consider that more than three quarters of the country's emissions come from household energy use, it becomes apparent that all we need to do to reach that goal is to double or triple the price homeowners pay for kilowatt-hours.

As of this writing, we are three weeks into the Russian invasion of Ukraine. On account of this event alone, energy prices are surging all over the globe. When you look at our current rate of inflation, then combine that with our commitment to reducing emissions by half in the next eight years, and then, finally, add to that the stress of cutting off Russian oil and gas from the world energy markets, it becomes impossible to predict how soon homeowners' energy costs will double or triple. However, it seems safe to predict that it will happen much sooner than the 15 years we've been predicting in our solar proposals, which have been compelling enough.

The reason why a homeowner should go solar is to remove inflation from the picture. They can fix the cost of their home's energy usage over the next 25 to 40 years without increasing their expenditures by one dollar. They can put solar on their home with a zero-dollar upfront cost and procure the power their family needs for a lower monthly payment than they are currently paying. I cannot think of a product that has a story as compelling as this one.

In addition to inflation, the cost of all the capital investments needed to modernize a hundred-year-old grid, enabling it to keep pace with distributed energy sources, storage, and security, will need to be priced into the future cost of electricity to homeowners. I had an enlightening conversation with a senior executive at a major utility company in my state who had become a customer. When he had me come to his house to show him solar, I thought he was punking me. I was thinking, *There must be a hidden camera. He's going to get me to say that we think prices are going to go up 4 to 5 percent over the next 15 years and that the cost of his company's power is going to double in 15 years. I'm going to end up on Channel 12 News.* He actually signed up that night with very few questions. Afterwards, we had become friends and were out in the desert riding our dune buggies. Alone together out in the middle of the desert, I asked him, "Now that you're all signed up and have our solar system, I'm just curious as to what you thought of my proposal and the projections that showed your power would double over the next 15 years." He responded, "Mike, I actually think your numbers are way off. I think the inflation numbers are about right, but you're completely missing the boat on the capital expenditures that will be needed to upgrade the grid to keep pace with security needs and renewable energy. Storage is going to be huge. I don't think the cost will double in 15 years; I'm pretty sure it will at least triple."

If you go to www.modsalesacademy.com, you can find information sources and handy tools, including charts and graphs to illustrate the effects of inflation, at both historical rates and projected higher rates.

The Benefits of Ownership vs. the Trap of Renting

Acquiring assets that appreciate over time using other people's money (OPM) is how rich people get wealthy. Most of the wealth that a middle-class person amasses over a lifetime comes from a home, an appreciating asset they acquired using a mortgage (OPM), and they paid down that mortgage over time, increasing their equity every month. They serviced that "debt" with money they were going to spend anyway as a housing expense. This strategy, using money one already has to acquire an appreciating asset instead of throwing that money out the window on a rental expense, is a perfect and direct corollary to the financial strategy behind going solar.

They have the ability to acquire and own a power plant using other people's money. The transaction requires zero upfront cash, and they're going to service the monthly payment with money they were going to spend anyway on what is essentially a rental expense. They are currently renting power equipment from their local electric utility. They don't have the slightest idea what they're going to be paid for that power over the next 10 to 30 years. My friend Bryce Felker with Voltaic calls it a "lifetime variable lease." The only thing they can be certain of is that the cost will relentlessly go up over time. Given the current circumstances with inflation and surging energy prices, they could find that price going up dramatically and quickly.

One of the primary benefits homeowners realize is one they don't really think about much. Because they have a fixed-rate mortgage, their monthly payment will be exactly the same in 10, 20, and 30 years. They have effectively removed inflation from the financial formula for their household expenses. The payment doesn't change over the term, except that when they get to 30 years the payment changes dramatically. It goes to zero. The house will be paid off, and their monthly recurring cost, excluding insurance and taxes, will be zero for the rest of their life.

If they redirect their monthly energy expense away from the local monopoly utility and toward a power plant that they have acquired, their monthly payment will be the same for the next 10 to 20 years and then drop to zero. They will have a zero monthly expense for electricity for the rest of their life. That solar system's production will degrade slightly over the next 25 years, but that will most likely be balanced by the increasing efficiency of their new major appliances.

What we are selling is energy security. Owning a home assures that they will be able to afford that home many years from now. But if they do not secure their energy cost, they may not be able to afford to continue living in that home. "Mr. Homeowner, could you afford to live here if it cost $9,000 a year instead of $3,000 a year to heat and cool it?" By owning their own power plant and fixing the cost, they now have energy independence, which will provide them with energy security.

The price of homes in the Arizona market have nearly doubled in the last several years. I love to talk to homeowners about this because they have benefited greatly from their decision to own during this time. I like to point out that if they had decided to rent this home a few years ago instead of purchasing it, they would have missed out on all that appreciation and equity. Not only that, but the landlord would be knocking on the door instead of a solar guy with a huge rent increase. I will ask them, "Given the current price your home would go for now, could you afford to purchase this home today?" In many cases the answer is no. In other words, if they had decided to wait awhile and see what happens, they would be looking at much less of a home in a different neighborhood. They would be experiencing profound regret! That is an easy segue to discussing what may happen if they decide to wait awhile before pulling the trigger on going solar.

All homeowners are playing a game. The game is to work 30 to 40 years and pay off a home, all the while putting 3 to 5 percent of their annual salary into a 401(k) and hoping to God to have enough money to maintain the lifestyle they had while they were working. Will this work? There is a constant anxiety that the variables in the equation will change over time, their plan will fail, and they will lose the game.

Given the current inflation rate, that concern is transforming into fright. There is a flight to security. People are selling stocks and buying gold. That flight to security should absolutely include locking in the price they will be paying for power over the next 10 to 30 years. They can secure all the power they will need while realizing significant savings over current prices. Not doing this while they can is arguably reckless. "Imagine, Mr. Customer, that you not only pay off your home in the next 20 to 30 years but also pay off your solar equipment, leaving you with zero monthly cost for your two biggest homeowner expenses." You may have thought before that you were knocking on doors to suggest an improvement that would lower a homeowner's monthly bill enough for them to eat out at Applebee's every month. In fact, what you really had to offer was a strategy for them to win the whole ball game.

When a homeowner buys a home, they have to come up with a down payment to create a small amount of equity in the beginning. With solar, the federal government gives them a 26-percent subsidy, which they can use as the down payment, creating immediate equity.

It's not about savings at all. I don't even cover the monthly savings in a solar presentation. It's not relevant to the conversation. What's relevant to the conversation is that it costs less, not more. It pays off the balance, and you become an owner instead of maintaining your status as a renter. We're talking about fixed cost, equity, appreciation and security.

Part 5

The 7-Figure Close

Chapter 15
Overcoming Objections

If a customer is voicing objections to moving forward with your product, that's good news. It means they are interested and are sharing the concerns that are pulling their mind in the other direction. If they weren't interested, they would have no objections because they're really not considering the proposal. They are asking for more information. Objections are actually buying questions, and they need to be treated correctly. In his book *See You at the Top,* Zig Ziglar teaches us that you cannot change people's minds; rather, you must offer them new information and then ask them to make a new decision. Arguing with the customer not only does little good; it usually pushes them away and gets them to dig in their heels in opposition.

We are dealing with a variety of specific concerns, but for the most part they all boil down to fear and greed. They are afraid of making a mistake. They are afraid of making a bad decision by signing up for a 25-year contract. They are also concerned that this might be a scam—that you are not what you make yourself out to be. Maybe you are not who you say you are. In many instances, they've just met you because you knocked on their door yesterday. Perhaps you've screwed a bunch of people out of their money, and they ended up with a new solar bill on top of the electric bill they had. They don't yet have sufficient reason to trust you, and they are just afraid that you may not really be 100-percent truthful with them. Many people have been in a car dealership after saying, "Honey, we are just going to go look at the car," and ended up with a new car and a new payment that night. That may or may not have worked out well for them. Many consumers have been to a timeshare presentation after saying, "We are just going to go get the weekend at a nice resort," and the next thing they know, they are sitting with this stone-cold killing machine whose company is adept at employing psychological warfare to get their signature on a contract today. So their objection may only be that they have a battle plan to avoid making a mistake. You are battling fear from past experiences.

The larger, overarching concern that you're dealing with at a solar presentation is that it just seems "too good to be true." Everyone has heard the adage that if something seems too good to be true, then it is probably not true. I like to bring this up in a solar presentation and explain to the customer that the main reason solar seems too good to be true is that the government injects a huge amount of money into the project, which skews all the numbers. On top of that, we are implementing a solution that provides free access to a commodity for which they currently pay a tremendous amount of money. There is no cost for solar energy. There is no way to put a meter on the sun, so this valuable commodity that they pay through the nose for is now something that they're getting at no cost. Of course, solar equipment is not free, but the monthly cost of it is less than what they are currently paying for the same utility. In addition to the equipment being subsidized and the commodity being free, it is also untaxed in most markets. They are used to paying something close to double the cost of that commodity because of local, county, state, and federal taxes and fees. Because solar energy is free, the equipment comes with no sales tax in most markets, and the monthly payment has no use tax, there is another hard-to-understand gap in cost.

I like to prepare them, often in the opening frame, that what I'm about to present to them will appear too good to be true, and I will cover the above reasons for why it seems that way while being absolutely true.

It is very important to isolate the actual objections. Customers will often throw out objections that are not really concerning them. They are merely smokescreens.

Often the customer throws out a standard objection that is not really his primary concern. You don't want to spend a lot of time addressing an issue that's not really holding them back. I am a student in my friend Brad Lea's sales-training course, which is called Closers School. He teaches a very effective method for isolating objections that he calls the magic wand. When the customer throws out a standard objection, he uses the magic wand to find out if it's their true concern. "I don't think solar is a good idea because I don't know how long I will be in this home." I reply: "I can understand that. Let's say you had a magic wand you could use to see the future, and you knew you were going to be in this home for the next 25 years. Would you then feel comfortable moving ahead with the solar project?" If he says yes, then we know we need to address that objection in earnest. If he says instead, "Well, no. Even if I knew I was going to live here a long time, I wouldn't want to go $40,000 in debt to take care of my electric bill." Me: "I hear what you're saying. Hypothetically, if we had a magic wand and you had $40,000 in the budget to pay cash for solar, would you feel as though this was a good investment and that you should move forward?"

What I'm really asking them is this: if we were able to solve that objection right now, would you have any other objections? I'm trying to get past the "smokescreen objections" and get to the real objections. Continue to use this method until you uncover their actual primary concern.

Another way to isolate the objection can be used during the Columbo Close, which we're going to cover in the next chapter. You let them off the hook and agree to give them time to think about it. When the pressure is off, you can then ask them, "Mary, after I leave and you and Bill are talking about this, what will be the one big thing you bring up as the reason you should hold off on going solar?" Or I'll say, "Bill, what about you? When you and Mary are breaking this down, what do you think will be your primary concern with respect to getting the solar system installed? You might as well take advantage of having the expert here at the table in case I can shed light on either of those concerns."

ISOLATE OBJECTIONS

- AFTER I LEAVE...WHAT WILL BE THE ONE THING THAT YOU WILL BRING UP?
- WHAT IS STOPPING YOU FROM TAKING ACTION?
- Hypothetically if we had a magic wand.........would you feel good about moving forward?

Salesmen tell, and stories sell. A story is a place where information and wisdom are stored and handed down. Stories are the primary way we passed down knowledge in the centuries before widespread literacy. Everyone loves a good story, and we are conditioned to receive new ideas and lessons from them. Telling a story is my favorite way to overcome an objection because it gives me tremendous latitude. Because I'm a salesman, they are worried that I may say whatever it takes to make them happy, so anything I *tell* them is subject to scrutiny. However, I can tell them a story about someone who was in a similar situation as them and had the same concern. With a story, I can bring an expert into the room who will share information and wisdom to address their specific concern, and they not only enjoy the story but are able to receive that information because it's not from the salesman.

Think of Leonardo DiCaprio's character in the movie *Inception*, a story about a team of people who use a device to participate in their subjects' dreams as they sleep. The fantastic action scenes in that movie revolve around one mission: to place a new idea into someone's mind.

SALESMAN TELL, STORIES SELL - USE A STORY

1. A story is a place that information and wisdom are stored
2. A story is an entertaining way to convey an idea
3. A story is an effective way to have someone in their position address their concern
4. Use a story to bring an expert into the meeting
5. Use a story to replace the idea in their head with they one you want them to have instead.........Inception

All objections can be handled with a basic framework. This can take many different forms and sound different based on how you approach it, but in the end, we are going to overcome all objections with a solution called the Three F's: *feel, felt,* and *found.*

"I Think Solar is Ugly"

We're going to start out by appearing to agree with the customer about their objection. Customer: "I really like the idea of solar, but I don't like the way it looks, and aesthetics are important to me." You: "Mary, I com-

pletely understand how you **feel** about that. Aesthetics are very important, especially with your home. Your home is your castle." This appears
to be an agreement with her objection, but what we're actually doing is
empathizing with her and how she feels.

You: "Mary, my next-door neighbor has a beautiful home, and she
felt exactly the same way. We talked about solar when I first moved in,
and she has wanted solar for several years. But her concerns about how
she thought the panels would look on her roof kept her from getting the
system." Now I am validating how she feels by telling her about someone
whom I have high esteem for and who felt the same way.

"After seeing the system on my house from her backyard, as well
as numerous other systems around the neighborhood, this is what she
found out." Now I am going to introduce new information, and it will
come not from me but rather someone who is in the same situation as
Mary and agrees with her objection. Notice that I haven't actually agreed
with her.

"While at first the sight of the panels was objectionable to her, she
realized that after a very short period of time she didn't take notice of
them at all. Then, after seeing many of them go up around the neighborhood—especially the new triple-black panels that look pretty sleek
because they do not have those annoying plaid lines—she discovered
that she mostly didn't notice all the solar in the neighborhood, and when
she did, it seemed that it was becoming the new normal. In the end,
she realized that if she was going to be looking at solar panels on homes
anyway, she might as well get the benefits of them. She had me install
the system on her home, and she has ended up very happy with the way
it looks." Then I show her a picture of her beautiful home with the new,
all-black, slim and sleek panels. "Mary, can you see why, after all was said
and done, she ended up putting the system on her home?"

What they are afraid of:

What solar looks like designed and installed properly today.

<u>"I'm going to move someday."</u>
"I can see why many families would go solar, and I think we would as

well, but we really don't know how long we're going to be living in this home." This can be handled very simply like this: "John, I understand exactly how you **feel**. Not only that, but most of our customers **felt** the same way. In reality, no one knows how long they will be in their current home. Let me tell you what they found out when they looked into it. Everyone will be moving someday. They are going to come for you with either a moving van or a hearse right? All kidding aside, though, it turns out that families on average move every eight years, and when they do, the electric bill *always* goes to the next person who acquires the property. It works the same way with solar. Your solar loan (or lease) is fully assumable. When your home is sold, it will simply pass to the buyer as any electric bill would. I am sure they will be delighted that the electric bill they are getting is significantly less than the one they would be getting from the utility if you did not go solar, and they will be thrilled to find out you have paid off eight years of their loan instead of having thrown that money away."

I will often show the customer an article from Zillow reporting that homes are selling for 4.1 percent more with solar than without. That's an independent source with lots of information and data about people selling their homes. I also like to point out that, out of our 8,000 customers with solar on their homes, on average about 20 of them a month change hands. The same thing happens every single time. The solar stays on the home. The loan or lease also stays with the home. Their name comes off the loan or lease, which means they are no longer liable, and the new homeowner's name goes onto the loan or lease. Neither our current homeowner nor the future homeowner has to pay off the loan or lease. This addresses their primary fear: that when they sell, they'll have to pay off the loan, which will come out of the profit from the sale. But why would somebody pay off the next person's electric bill for the next 20 years? That is not the way it works.

"What if the new buyer doesn't want the system?"

"Mary, I can understand why you would **feel** anxious about that. In fact, my good friend Robert went solar with us and then realized that he had to move for his job two years later. He **felt** nervous that the new buyer might not want solar. What he **found** out was, his realtor listed the property as a solar home, just as he would have listed a pool or any other amenity, and the buyer's real-estate agents only brought people who were fine with that. People who don't want a pool only look at homes that don't have one. In fact, his realtor listed his home on GreenHomesFor-Sale.com, and they ended up selling the home to a customer who saw that listing and would not have bought a home without solar.

"Wouldn't it be safer to let the new buyer put solar on himself?"

"I can definitely understand why you would **feel** that would be the safe bet. I was just trying to help a previous homebuyer who was moving forward with a solar design for a home he was looking to purchase in Tucson. The existing homeowner had looked at solar several times but **felt** too uncertain about their future plans. As it turns out, the State of Arizona has set a cap on how many homes can connect a solar system to the grid, and their particular neighborhood had already surpassed the 15-percent maximum. I wasn't able to provide a solar solution for the new buyer, and he ended up choosing a home in a neighborhood that already had solar. The existing seller found out that they had missed the opportunity for their home to go solar and that it could not be sold to people who felt they needed it."

"I want solar, but I don't want to take on any debt."

This objection is very common but often unstated. It will sometimes come up when someone calls to cancel after signing up. They get a hard case of buyer's remorse and become very anxious about taking on debt.

"Jason, I understand exactly how you **feel**. My brother Joe is a big Dave Ramsey fan, and he was determined to pay cash for solar. He talked to his financial planner and CPA about taking the money out of his portfolio to pay cash, and this is what he **found** out: he was using the bank's money with no out-of-pocket cost and a low-interest, long-term loan that worked exactly like a mortgage on a house. Everyone would love to pay cash for a home and not have a mortgage, but that would mean getting a much smaller home or waiting a long time before they bought one. Instead of doing either of those things, they would be better off using the mortgage company's money to acquire a nicer home sooner and then using the money that they would have spent on rent to pay off the mortgage. That way, you would create equity while owning a bigger home sooner and experiencing much more appreciation as the market goes up. In fact, Joe found out that because the government was putting up the down payment in the form of the 26-percent tax credit, he was walking into an immediate equity position with no down payment, which was going to cause his net worth to go up, not down. He was acquiring not debt but rather equity. This is how the wealthy get wealthy. They use other people's money to acquire assets that appreciate over time and then service the loan with money they would have had to pay anyway."

<u>"I want to get two or three more quotes."</u>

"John, I understand exactly how you **feel**. When I make a significant purchase, I want to make sure I'm getting a good deal. I was working with Joshua, one of my best friends from high school, and we had the perfect solar design for his home. Joshua manages purchasing for a big defense contractor, and he **felt** the same way you do. He told me, 'Mike, even though we are great friends and you know I'm going to buy the system from you, I feel I would be professionally negligent if I didn't put the project out to bid.'

"Well, let me tell you what he **found** out. The first thing he did was push the button on the Internet that says 'get three quotes for solar in your area.' He discovered this was not an actual solar company but a marketing company that sold leads to every solar company in town. He proceeded to get several quotes, and, yes, he found some that were lower and some that were higher. Being an experienced purchasing professional, he knew to throw out the high bid and the low bid. There was a spread between the rest, but it was one you could throw a blanket over. The companies that were less expensive than mine had lower ratings, and he ended up not feeling very comfortable with having them drill more than a hundred holes in his roof. The ones that were more expensive were smaller boutique firms that didn't really have any volume and needed to make a lot more money per job. My company does very significant volume, but it is also a real company with actual engineers and customer-service people.

What he **found** was that my price was at the low end of the middle, which is exactly where he was trying to end up. However, he also discovered that he had ended up in the crosshairs of 20 solar companies. He was getting calls at all hours, emails in all of his inboxes, and even finding people waiting for him in his driveway when he came home from work. He told me that when trying to choose between several contractors, what you're really looking for is the best contractor's best price. What you don't want is the worst contractor's lowest price."

I then moved into an "if I could, would you" close, which is covered in detail in the next chapter. "John, what I have shown you here in my proposal is our standard pricing. My mom went solar with us, and to be honest, she got our best price. If I could get you approved for the same pricing my mom got and get you a shortcut to the best contractor's best price, could we get this written up tonight?"

<u>"I don't want anything done to my roof."</u>

"Art, It makes sense that you are concerned about the integrity of your roof. I understand exactly how you **feel**. The last thing in the world you need is to be worrying every time it rains. In fact, my neighbor is a general contractor, and he had the same concerns and **felt** the same way. Let me tell you what he **found** out." Then I'm going to back up and start addressing our roof-installation process and the roof-penetration warranty.

<u>"My roof needs to be replaced first."</u>

"Janet, I understand exactly how you feel. The last thing you would want is to install a solar system and then have to take it down to put on a new roof a year or two later. My son's teacher was holding off on solar because her roof needed to be replaced. She **felt** that while she was gathering the funds to do the roof, it would be best to wait on solar. What she **found** out was that we could put the roofing project into the 25-year, low-interest financing of the solar system and do both projects at the same time with no money out of pocket. Now she has a brand-new roof with a solar system in place, and her monthly payment is about the same as what she was paying for just the electric bill. On top of that, there were several other projects on her wish list for which she was able to use the roof money.

This process is the same for any product or service. The primary thought to keep in mind is that the benefits of the product are so powerful that they alone will overcome most objections. In the case of solar, the positive cash flow, profits, and appreciating home value are all tremendously compelling. But even these pale in comparison to the idea that the customer, by virtue of owning their own power plant, is going to have energy independence. This independence is going to provide energy security. That is compelling in normal times, but in times of high inflation, rising interest rates, and surging energy costs, it is absolutely essential. This outweighs any concerns about aesthetics or additional tasks for their realtor when they sell their home.

Address the customer's concerns and objections with the Three F's. Bring an expert into the room by way of an interesting and dramatic story. Elicit a nod by asking them, "Does this make sense?" Then move forward by revisiting the compelling benefits of solar, especially the security that providing three or four decades' worth of power at a lower and fixed cost will bring to their family.

Chapter 16
The Master Closer Mindset

I'm going to help you to adopt the mindset needed to close the sale today. It's very important for you to understand that this is your primary purpose and objective. This is the entire reason you are being sent to this customer's home. It is your actual job.

Everybody's been in a car salesman's office, and most people have been in a timeshare presentation. They've experienced the high-pressure close. They're worried that they've invited somebody into their home who is about to execute a high-pressure close right there at their kitchen table, and they're going to react by being reluctant to commit. So the very first thing you want to do is to think about this reluctance just like another objection and treat it as such. Don't let your little heart break when a customer says they want to think about it. Instead, you need to hear the bell ringing outside the boxing ring. It's time to go to work.

This is not an adversarial situation. It's a game of psychological warfare to some degree, but it really can be a friendly thing all the way around. One of the reasons salespeople don't want to pull the hammer out of the bag is that they are afraid it's going to get awkward. I'm telling you: it's never awkward. When someone tries to do their job, they've already told you what their job is. Now you're going to try to get your job done. Your job is to show the customer the product, answer all their questions, and then get the process started.

I believe that in order to serve the customer at the highest level, you must do more than educate and inform the customer; you must help them make the decision to take the next step—today.

As we discussed, this is the only meeting that you're going to have with this customer. It is the only opportunity to get paid for the hours of work that you've put in to get to this point. That includes all the no's at the door and all the no-sale presentations. If you're at the table and they're at the table, you have a very good chance, certainly the best chance you'll ever get to close this sale and serve the customer. If you're not selling a product that you absolutely believe will benefit this customer, and if you're not working for a company you know is superior to their other choices, then quit today and find a product and a company that you are 100-percent certain meet those conditions.

The fact of the matter is that in solar sales, you and I are not really needed. Solar sells itself. There is no upfront cost; the monthly payment is less than they are already paying; the federal government gives them a huge amount of money because we are helping the planet in an epic way; and with the new kind of inflation we're experiencing and with the Green New Deal, they are likely making a tragic mistake if they don't go solar. We could easily get all that across in a YouTube video. The reason we are sending a motivated, heat-seeking missile with a supercomputer attached (you) is that you and I are absolutely needed for that moment when the customer says this: "Wow, why the heck hasn't everyone gone solar already? It should be a law that everyone has to go solar! I want to go solar…on a different day than today, after I think about it for a few days."

The person in that meeting who needs to be 100-percent certain there is never going to be another meeting is you. Salesmen are sent to present and educate. Closers are sent to a meeting to help the customer overcome their fear of making a decision. Their job is to help the customer pull the trigger. The company could have sent a YouTube video via email to explain the features and benefits and get the customer interested. But instead, they sent a human supercomputer with empathy and intuition to navigate the maze of subterfuge, indecision, and fear so that all the money spent to launch this missile at the target would result in the missile hitting the bullseye.

It's not about your commission. Serving the customer and getting your job done: that's what you get paid for. That's why you were sent to this meeting. It is absolutely essential that you have the courage to use the tools that you've brought to the meeting in your toolbox. The customer is counting on you. They did not invite you to the kitchen table where they make decisions so that you could lose heart and chicken out. The company is counting on you. They did not spend all that money on marketing and training so that you could spend two hours with a customer and then not have the guts to use the tools to get the job done.

Now is your moment! Let's say things are going well. It feels as though a sale is in progress, and then the prospect says, "Can you email this to me? Can I have all this awesome information so that I can start a study project and devote the next few weeks of my life to validating all this info? I was busy with my job and life when you got here, but now I can see that this needs to be a priority, and I'm going to get right on it." I think I can hear your little heart breaking right now. Well, it shouldn't. We have arrived at the stage of the process where you are the most important person in the industry. This is where you go to work and provide maximum value. It is time for you to get out your tool box and *go to work* and stay at it until the job is done!

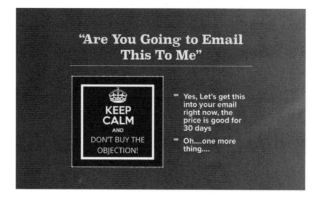

This is what closers do. Not everyone is cut out to be or wants to be a closer. It is not the only style of selling. A closer is like a hunter who will either take down prey or will go hungry. Many salespeople are not hunters but farmers. I was in business-to-business sales for over 20 years, and it frustrated me that there really weren't many opportunities to close a sale. It was a follow-up-and-build-relationships sales model. You interacted with numerous people who worked for a corporation until a purchase order ended up in your email inbox three to nine months later.

But there is no reason why you can't be a closer—if you want to.

I have talked about these tools for years with some of the same people in my own organization, and I know that they don't use them even though they've seen them work countless times. Why is that? Why would someone look at a nail, look down at the hammer in their toolbox, and then decide to leave the hammer in the toolbox, hoping that somehow the job will get done after he leaves when there is no one there to do it?

The answer is that he knew that if he grabbed the hammer, it would make things awkward.

I have a very good salesperson who works for me. I have been telling him about this toolbox for five years, but it's not for him. He meets with prospects, and they become seeds in the field that he is farming. He tends to this field, and he produces sales over time. When I ask him why he doesn't pull the hammer out of the toolbox when he sees a nail, he says, "I don't want to be *that* guy. I don't want to come across like a used-car salesman. If I pull out that hammer, it's going to get really awkward."

And you know what? He is absolutely right! When the customer says, "I want to think about it," and instead of buying the objection you go to work doing your job as a closer, which is to make an alternate proposal, it is going to get at least a little awkward. The farmer doesn't want to risk all the rapport he has built up by challenging the customer's proposal, which is to stop the meeting and try to start it again on a different day, with his own proposal, which is to consider a reason to continue today and then to go to the next step. In truth, one of the reasons why I say that I am not coming back is that, after I apply my skills and my willpower to the situation and it doesn't work, it actually is awkward. There is not a great deal of rapport left to use for further meetings. The walk to the door is not a happy one for anyone in the meeting. I am usually better off handing the opportunity over to my guys who do come back. And that is what I do.

Remember: this is essentially a contest of wills. They want to put this off, and you want to make the sale. People ask me who makes a great closer, and my answer is somebody who does what they need to do to get their way *most* of the time. You want to be *that* person.

It's time to get over your fear of the awkwardness. It's time to find the courage to step out onto what appears to be a rickety rope bridge across a deep and forbidding chasm. What exactly are we afraid of? What's the very worst thing that can happen other than the awkwardness? We're back to where we started: our primal fear of rejection. It's not rational. Obviously, a few more minutes of conversation is worth turning the last two hours into a very productive encounter for you, the company, and the customer.

It doesn't make any sense, yet it happens over and over again. It's why most companies in my industry have a sit-to-closing ratio of between 10 and 20 percent. It's why people believe a 30-percent closing ratio is par for the course. They don't realize that most of their salespeople are quitting at the very moment that they have the very best chance of success. The reason is fear.

If you are a farmer and you "don't want to be *that* guy," that's OK. If you are happy with the yield from farming, then the rest of this course is not for you. You can make good money in sales and in solar with that approach. The problem is that if you see most people two or three times, you will cut down the number of people you can see by between a third and a half. If you come back tomorrow night, that means you will not be with another prospect tomorrow night in that slot, which will cost you potentially thousands of dollars. The money that pays for the incentives to move forward today will dwarf the loss from having fewer opportunities to close and do more prospecting. The very small number of people who would have bought later if you hadn't pressed is nothing compared to the number of people you will help if you spend that time prospecting and blazing forward.

If you do want to be a closer but get a little nauseous thinking about using tactics that some mistakenly consider "high pressure," you must overcome this concern and get comfortable with being in a room that you have caused to become awkward. What do you have to lose? When you come to terms with the real odds of making the sale once you leave the room, you will understand that you have nothing to lose and everything to gain, including a happy and grateful customer. I have done this thousands of times, and I can tell you from experience that the happiest person in the room after a sale has been closed is the customer, who has just gotten over their fear and hesitancy and agreed to move forward. It goes from awkward to a buyer's party! They don't have a follow-up project. They have the benefits of the product to enjoy. They feel relaxed and happy that they received a high level of professional service.

Knowing this, what would make you choose not to use these tools? The biggest reason is that you agree that they really do need more time— that they need to do this on a day that's not today. Somehow, magically, between now and that day, they are going to have more information and be more ready. Do *not* do this. Do *not* buy this objection. It is not true. The opposite is usually true. And if it does end up true, it's because they talked to more salespeople, and one of them was a better closer than you. They are going to get the business, not you. So if you really believe that something is going to happen between now and next Friday that will make them ready to make a decision, you are the one who's going to be disappointed.

Let's say someone says this to you: "Hey, you're awesome. This is the way to go. *You* are my guy for sure. There is zero chance I'm not doing this. I just want to do it on a day that's not today. I just need until tomorrow morning, so come back to my house at nine o'clock." I am telling you from experience that 99 times out of 100, you're going to get a call at 8:30 with news that their mom is sick and they are hopping on a plane, so please don't come. Once you leave, the spell is broken. The magic is gone. The urgency isn't there. They think, "Why did this seem urgent last night? Why did it seem like I needed to get this figured out in the next 24 hours when I could just wait a while?" That's what happens almost every time.

What is the secret to finding the courage at that moment? It's the understanding and the belief that there is not going to be another meeting. "I'm not coming back": I actually say that to customers. I don't say it because I'm trying to be a jerk. I don't say it to be rude. I don't say it because it wouldn't be worth the time to come back to write up paperwork. I say it because it's a fact. *There is not going to be another meeting.* The number of times that a second meeting actually happens is a small enough number to call it zero. If I understand and believe that my very best chance to make this a win is in front of me now and will never be there ever again, then I can find the courage to grab my toolbox, put it on the table, and go to work.

Everything that has happened up to this point has merely been a precursor to bringing you to close at this moment. This moment is the culmination of hopes, dreams, and a lot of work. You're in your corner and have been through 12 rounds. Now the bell is ringing, and it's time to step up and finish this thing.

So you need to buy into two key ideas. Number one: you're not coming back. Farmers have better percentages for follow-up than I do because they don't ask for the order and they don't go through the process of closing. They miss out on a lot of people who would have bought today, and they get some of them to buy on a subsequent day because they were already sold. But many of those customers could have been sold in the first meeting. The other reason the farmers' follow-up percentages are better than mine is that I don't call them back. That's because I don't have time to chase opportunities that offer less than a one-in-ten chance. My closing ratio is typically seven or eight out of ten. I often close ten in a row. I frequently close three in a day. Why would I ever go backwards chasing opportunities that are one in ten, let alone one in 100, when I can keep moving forward and close 70 to 80 percent of the time? I wouldn't. I don't. That's why I am not coming back. I explain that to the customer in a way that makes good business sense and let him know that we have people for coming back. But that's not me.

For the customers who are not ready to commit, that's OK. We still want their business. As I said, we have people for that. They are called "the sales department."

"When this process is over, I am going to be either walking this project into the installation department or texting a lead to the sales department. I am not in that department, so I won't be the one who will be helping you in the future. *But*, if you are willing to commit, then I am your representative in the solar business, and I'm not going to let you fail. I'm going to stick with you. We are going to be on each other's speed dial until there is glass on your roof, it's working, and you're happy. In fact, I will be with you for many years to come. Why? Because I am not only here to save you money; I am here to make you money. You're going to make bank on every person you know who owns a house and wants to go solar. I am going to get them signed up in *the* meeting, and you're going to make $500 each time I do so!"

So that's number one: establishing that you're not coming back. Number two is understanding that your real job is to serve the customer, your company, yourself, and your family. You are there to be of service, and your job is to help the customer get over their fear so that they can start enjoying the benefits of what you're selling. If they don't, then for you it makes a difference for a minute; for the customer, it makes a difference for a lifetime. Either they are not going to take advantage of all the incentives, or they are going to buy from another company that is going to be nowhere near as good for them as yours would be. If you don't believe that passionately, then you cannot convey it. You can not transfer conviction that you don't have. If that is the case, you may not be working for the right company.

To provide the highest level of service, you must believe that you are letting the customer down unless you refuse to buy the objection that they need to do this on another day. You must be able to convey emphatically that they are truly better off if they take the next step *today*, and you must overcome the anxiety about using the tools in your toolbox by replacing it with a burning determination to do the right thing. You are not being *that* guy. Rather, you are serving the customer, your company, and your family.

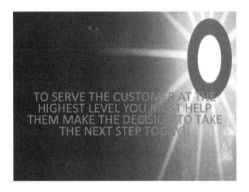

TO SERVE THE CUSTOMER AT THE HIGHEST LEVEL YOU MUST HELP THEM MAKE THE DECISION TO TAKE THE NEXT STEP TODAY!

My wife knows this. When I call her up and say, "I had a really good meeting, and they are sold on solar," she says, "Awesome, did you sign them up tonight?" If I say, "Nah, they say they need to talk to their realtor and their accountant, and they should be ready to sign by Friday or maybe Saturday," then, because she's a salesman's wife who has heard this story a thousand times, she knows the odds of a be-back better than I do. She *knows* that be-backs don't make mortgage payments. She would say, "Yeah, well, it's late, so you should stop and get yourself something to eat, and maybe sleep out on the couch so you don't wake me up." What she's thinking is, *You were sent there to do a grown-up's job, and you've got a little boy's excuse for why you're coming home tonight with no bacon and a plan to waste another prime selling night chasing people who can't pull the trigger instead of helping another person who could make a decision, which would be good for their family and ours.* Yeah.

Let's say I call her up on the way home and tell her, "Honey, this family was really interested, and they seemed to really get it, and of course, like always, they wanted a few days to think about it. I really tried my best to help them overcome their hesitation. I overcame each of their objections. After I emailed them the proposal and told them, 'No pressure, folks, the price is good for 30 days.'

Then I really got into it and walked them through the "today only" close. I really put them through it and put them right onto the horns of the dilemma. He was ready, but she was still against it. We backed up and dealt with her concern about selling the house someday. I told her the story about our brother-in-law Rob. I moved into an 'If I could, would you..." close and still couldn't get them both there. So I really emptied the clip with the incentives and gave them the 'I'm here, you're here, so put me to work for you' speech. Then I did the 'some deal is better than no deal for my company' bit and handed them the pen. Honey, after all that, I could not help them overcome their anxiety about moving forward. Anyway, I told them that I really appreciated them spending the time with me, and I let them know that our follow-up team would stay in touch with them and that we would be ready to help them when they were ready."

When she hears that story, she says, "Way to get your job done, baby. I'll get dinner on the table and see you in a little bit." That's because I did everything I could to serve that family and ours.

One of the reasons why I don't call people back is because after I've gone through my process and gotten three or four no's, that walk to the front door is an awkward walk. It's like the walk of shame for me. I tried to get us to the finish line, and I couldn't do it. They're embarrassed, and I'm embarrassed. It's not good, and neither one of us is looking forward to spending more time together. So, if you want to create leads to farm, that's a different process. I'm not saying that's a bad process. I'm just saying that you're never going to get to seven figures in sales that way. You just can't do it. The way to do it is by constantly moving forward and helping people who are able to make a decision.

What if you do all you can and end up closing someone who didn't want to be sold? Well, first of all, they could cancel, and that's OK. My cancellation rate over five years has been somewhere between 10 and 15 percent. When I lose those people, I lose those people. That's just part of the numbers and part of the math. It's another way to get to no. But again, it's not a tragedy to sign up somebody who wasn't quite sold or later became unsold or fell into buyer's remorse. But it's an absolute tragedy to have somebody who is sold and doesn't become closed.

Chapter 17
Execution - Close the Door

You've made a friend. You've built the door frame. You're at the threshold. During the presentation, the structure has taken on depth and substance. It has been elaborated with color, texture, and ornamentation. It looks hopeful and joyful on the other side of that threshold. It's time to invite, and if necessary, carry the customer across the threshold.

I will routinely close five to ten in a row. I don't close 100 percent, but I'll get close to it. I close well over 200 solar deals a year, and I've closed over 300 in one year. And I did all that by overcoming every objection in the book.

But I want to reiterate that all the stuff we talked about leading up to the close is far more important. The close is easy; everything leading up to it is the hard part. But I'll show you what I do—and it works. You will close sales if you do the things that we talked about, but only if you're in enough appointments to do them. Four a day would be ideal. If you're in four appointments a day, you're going to be making a huge mid-six-figure income, and you're going to be loving life. The rest of it is just increasing your odds.

But when it comes to crossing the threshold, you have to transition from the presentation to the close. Part of that is asking questions, and the idea behind the questions is to find out if they're ready to jump into the boat. I'd say that at about 15 percent of presentations, they ask me what's next, and I say I just need their driver's license and we're in business. Those are the people who just step aboard, and probably anybody could have closed that deal. But most of the deals don't go that way.

Most of the time, you're winding through the presentation, which then includes a proposal. And that's when you start looking for objections:

So, are you ready to go?
Have you seen enough to start the process?
Have I given you enough information to start moving forward today?
Do you see the benefits?
Is this making sense to you?
Is there any reason that this would not make sense for you?
Of the two designs I showed you, which one makes the most sense to you?

CLOSING QUESTONS

- IT SEEMS LIKE THIS IS MAKING A LOT OF SENSE TO YOU. AM I RIGHT ABOUT THAT?
- IT FEELS LIKE GOING SOLAR IS MAKING A LOT OF SENSE. AM I RIGHT ABOUT THAT?
- IT SEEMS LIKE A PERFECT FIT FOR YOU, ARE YOU READY TO TAKE THE NEXT STEP?

When you're getting close, a great transition is to make them see it all in a broad perspective:

"Do you see the benefits?"

"Is there any reason this wouldn't make sense?"

"It seems like this is making sense to you. Am I right about that?"

There are a hundred different ways you can say that, and you need to find your way. Basically, you're just asking them, "are you ready to step into the boat?" And when they say, "Oh, are you going to email it to me?" you need to not have your little heart break. You need to think, *OK, now it's time to go to work. Now it's time to start really trying to close.*

"It seems like this is a perfect fit for you."
"So it seems like this is making sense."
"Are you ready to take the next step?"

There's a million ways to ask, "Are you ready to move forward?" This is all to get them to say, "You know, it does make a lot of sense." Except that they'll keep saying, "Yes, just not today," but you need to stay in the ring because the bell has not yet rung this match to a close.

We built this frame for a reason: to hold the door. Now we're going to close the door. You can also think of it as the gate of a corral. You're going to run them into this corral, and they're going to want to slip away by telling you that you're their guy, you're coming back, and we're all going to sign this and have this happy party on a different day. But you can't let that happen. You have to keep guiding them toward the gateway of the corral.

People will often ask me about the downsides, so be ready four that. I like to make a joke and tell them that the big downside with solar is that it performs awful at night! Another one is that the process takes time. It takes a lot of time to go from paperwork to glass on the roof, making power today with no utility bill. So we have to get the process started. That's my code word for signing paperwork.

In my industry, solar power, the customer is often signing a 25-year contract. So it's an invitation to a partnership that lasts much of a lifetime. Our proposal is exactly that: a proposal. Saying yes does not mean we're married, but it does mean we're engaged. Much has to be done to get from the threshold to being in a 25-year partnership. In a sense, we're getting married, but today the invitation is to start the process and announce to the world that we are engaged.

Every sales book you will read will tell you to ask for the order. I have never asked for the order. I invite the customer to take my hand and cross this threshold as we begin the process of realizing the benefits they now desire.

"Mr. Customer, will you take my hand and begin this journey? What are your thoughts about the proposal I have made? Are you ready to take my hand and move forward? Being that this proposal does not cost you money but rather makes you money, doesn't it make sense?"

At this point, you're typically going to hear something like this: "Are you going to email this proposal to me? How long can I wait and still be able to take advantage of these benefits?" And they have all the excuses you've heard before and will hear again.

An inexperienced salesperson—and often an experienced one—will hear this and experience the crushing weight of disappointment. The more sold a customer is, the more disappointing it is to hear them say that they definitely want to sign but want to do so on a day that is not today. They may have a reason, or they may have no reason. If, in fact, they are sold—and most salespeople can tell most of the time that the person is sold—then there is only one of several reasons why they are not jumping up and down to do paperwork right now. Ask more questions to find out what their objections are. Again, you're not going to change anybody's mind. What you're going to do is give them more information, and they're going to make a different decision. If they're not ready to move forward, find out why.

Keep educating them, but don't think you can teach them everything. You're transferring your confidence and conviction. As long as they know that I know everything about solar and am convinced that they're way better off with it, then they're going to go with it. They're never going to understand everything I understand, but they also want to know that I understand their objections.

They do not realize that it is in their best interest to say yes today. They have a strong instinct that their interests lie in procrastinating on big decisions. Sometimes that is the case. If you were a con man with a compelling scam, that would actually be true. If that is true, I hope you stop reading this book. But if you are selling a terrific product from an excellent company, it is not the case. They are never going to have this issue on the front burner more than it is now. They are never going to devote more time and attention to solving whatever problem your product overcomes than they are right now. The truth is that if they don't pull the trigger, they will most likely never come back to this point ever again. This instinct is working against them just as much as it is you. If your product truly delivers benefits that will enhance their life, now is the time to strike because the iron is hot.

The two primary reasons why they are not grabbing the pen are fear and greed.

Remember, they are afraid that you're a con man. They're not sure if the company is legit. It actually seems too good to be true. They remember the time they said yes to a free weekend at a timeshare resort, ended up in the clutches of a master closer, and then ended up owing decades' worth of payments for a product that brought them little benefit. They have been told that if something sounds too good to be true, then it is probably not true. If you are a good salesperson selling a great product, it may have the ring of "too good to be true." I will often tell a prospect that my proposal seems too good to be true, and here are the reasons why that is so.

The energy from the sun is absolutely free. They are paying thousands of dollars per year for a commodity they are being bathed in for free every day. Secondly, the federal government and many state governments provide massive cash subsidies via tax credits and rebates that truly make the math look wrong. They are not accustomed to getting money from the government. Successful homeowners are used to forking money over to the government and watching other people receive government benefits. So one of their primary concerns is that they could sign a contract and find out later that it's the company that's actually receiving the benefits they are hoping to receive. They want time to check you out and do research on the Internet.

The other side of that coin is greed. The customer thinks that maybe they can get a similar product from a similar company at a substantially lower price. In the solar business, I am often showing homeowners a system that has a sticker price of between $40,000 and $80,000, and sometimes as high as $100,000. If they were to take my proposal and shop at 25 other companies, is it possible that they could save $1,000? Could they save $10,000? Could they save $35,000? The answer is that they have no idea.

So they're afraid that there's either a better solution or a better price. Those are concerns that turn into objections about moving forward. All objections are handled with one basic framework, and that can take on a lot of different looks and feels depending on how you deal with it, but they can all be classified with a solution that is characterized by feel, felt, found.

So the last thing you want to do is once you've drawn out all the objections, you're going to back them off. They're going to shut down and quit telling you things. What you want them to do is tell you more. You're going to want to find out exactly what's wrong and come at them with feel, felt, found. It can take a lot of different formats as we talked about, but the best is with a story.

"I agree and understand exactly how you feel. Many of our customers felt the same way. Let me tell you what they found out with more information."

Let's say my customer is concerned about a potential leaking roof from the solar-panel installation. I tell them I understand the concern of having 100 holes in their roof, and I tell them about my brother who has the same concern and let me tell you what he found out... Then I'm going to go back up. I'm going to start addressing the roof warranty, the roof process, which I'd covered briefly, but now we're going to go into more detail. Because an objection is a request for more information, but we want to isolate a lot of the objections because most of them are fake. If you can get to the real ones, you can provide more information. And then I use what my friend Brad Lea calls the magic wand: "Hypothetically, if you knew your roof was never going to be a problem after going solar, would you be ready to start the process?"

The bottom line is that you are the expert. You are the one that knows where the market is. It's time to be forthcoming and explain to the customer where the market is and what they could find if they were to go out into the marketplace and hold a beauty contest or bake off.

The Time has Come for "The Close"
We have built the frame, and in the presentation we have hung the door.

We have used trial closes to see if they are already prepared to step over the threshold. In most cases, these have caused them to reveal their concerns and objections. We've used the magic wand to isolate the objection. "If you had a magic wand and you instantly knew you were going to live here forever, would you be comfortable moving forward?"

We used the Three F's. We told a story to overcome those true objections and have returned with another closing question. "It seems as if this is making a lot of sense to you both. Am I right about that?" You might even go right to the paperwork with an assumption close: "We just need to get you approved for the financing. Are you both listed on the deed to the home? And would you like us to have both of you on the paperwork?" Or: "Which one of you has the best credit? Should we put you down first on the application?"

If one of these closes does the trick, stop selling! It is important not to sell past the yes. Remain calm and move to the paperwork.

In most cases, though, you are going to hear something like: "Oh, yes. This makes total sense. We are just going to need a couple of days to go through everything. Are you going to email this to me?"

This is a pivotal moment! Don't pout or argue. You need to learn that this is a buying sign and treat it like any other objection. Remember: you cannot change people's minds. You can only give them new information and ask them to make a new decision. But first, let's let all the pressure out of the room so we can just talk.

It's time for the Columbo Close.

Columbo was a police detective who investigated murders on a television show from the 1970s. He always wore this old, wrinkly raincoat and had this somewhat annoying, but not intimidating, mostly friendly demeanor. He would be questioning a suspect and would appear to be buying their alibi, even agreeing that there's not much of a chance that they could have had the opportunity to murder the victim. That would have the effect of letting the suspect off the hook and removing all the pressure, which would be followed by more friendly banter.

"Yeah, no, no, I know. It definitely wasn't you."

He would pack up his briefcase, walk to the door, grab the handle, and stop for one second. Then he would turn back around and say, "You know, Bill, there is just one more thing. Just one more thing that's bothering me. Between 10 o'clock when you left your office and 11:30 when you got home, there's this 35-minute period that's unaccounted for. And I just can't figure out, you know. What happened? Where were you during those 35 minutes? Can you help me understand that?" The guy always sweats and confesses, and a few minutes later, he's in handcuffs.

You may or may not be aware of it, but during a sales presentation with a smooth professional closer, the prospect is often very nervous and on guard. There can be quite a bit of pressure in the room, which comes from the conflict between the sales person's desire to make the sale and the prospect's desire to procrastinate. So this very same tactic can be used.

I like to tell the customer at this point, "Absolutely, I can email this proposal to you. This is the free estimate that we promised you. Let's get that into your email inbox right now. Is there anybody you'd like me to copy on it? Your accountant or lawyer or your dad? What's the best email address to send that to? Oh, by the way, the pricing in the proposal, which is now in your inbox, is good for 30 days. No pressure, folks."

Then I start folding up my iPad and putting stuff away. I let all the pressure out of the room. The first thing I'm going to do is help them to understand that I really do want them to have "all the time in the world" to make sure that this is the right decision for them.

"By the way, how much time are we talking about? We're talking about weeks, months, a couple of days?" At this point the customer will become very expressive and insistent that they are just a few days from having you back to do paperwork. They want to make you feel as if your time with them has been productive, as if you haven't wasted your time.

"Oh, no, you've convinced me. I'm going to be ready by Friday."

"Awesome. Friday, two days from now. Perfect. Now that we have covered everything and the proposal is in your email, let's talk about what your real concerns may be. You've got the expert here in the room, and I've seen everything. I have helped over a thousand families figure out if this was the right thing for them. Mary, after I'm gone and you and Bill are talking about this, what's going to be the one big thing that's giving you a reason to pause? What about you, Bill, as you and Mary are discussing this over the next day or so, what's the major concern you have that would keep you from moving forward?"

Get ready to really listen and to hear some things that may be very surprising. They've been holding the real reason that's holding them back, and perhaps even the other spouse doesn't know what that is. I was once at this point in the process with a middle-aged couple when the wife announced: "Bill doesn't know this, but I have a realtor coming tomorrow. The last of our five children have gone off to college, and I believe we need to move out of this big house and into a smaller one, and if I have my way, this house will be up for sale by the end of the week." Now, there are two reasons a customer will not move forward. The first is an objection and the second is a condition. It is your job to overcome objections, but there's nothing you can do about a condition. This particular presentation came to a pretty abrupt end, and there was a "for sale" sign in the yard a few days later.

One lady announced at this point that she was afraid that if her husband had solar, he would turn the AC down and use up all the solar power the system was going to provide, so there would not be enough power leftover to run her deep freezer. She was afraid she would lose all her frozen food. It was hard not to join her husband in looking at her as if she had two heads. Anyone who knows the first thing about how a solar system works would know that the concern she had was absurd. But that doesn't matter. It's what was concerning her, and she was against the project. I sat back and let her husband explain to her that they would have an unlimited amount of power no matter how much air conditioning he used and that there was no way her freezer could possibly go without power. At that point she became very relaxed and deferred to her husband. "You know best, dear. If you're comfortable signing up for solar, so am I."

Now that we have the real objection, we can use the Three F's and tell them one of the stories that overcomes their particular concern. Now it's time to get them to make a new decision. It's time for the "Today Only" Close.

Now I'm going to try to drill down to the real objection. "What's stopping you from moving forward today?" Whatever it is, I'm going to agree with it, and I'm going to understand it. And then I'm going to share a story that provides information that can help them make a different decision. And then I'm going to move on to the "Today Only" Close.

"The reason this is a 'today only' offer is because I'm not coming back. I'd love to come back in the morning, but unfortunately, my calendar is completely full. Remember, my job is to meet with three or four new families every day. I'm not the guy who comes back. But don't worry: we've got a bunch of salesmen, and one of them will take great care of you. And he'll be glad to have another customer he can make commission on. You know, we're kind of in it for the commission, but I'm in here to try and help you get the process started."

Then I share a story with them. That story is going to be about why it's unbelievably important for me to start the process. And another story about why it's unbelievably important for them--everything they'll be losing out on. Have reasons why it makes tremendous sense to get the process started today. And if we were able to do that, then I think I could craft something that would be a win-win solution.

It's a win for you because you get the sale, and you can say that, but you need to explain why it's a win for them. "Here's the story on why it's a perilously bad idea not to move forward on this today. But let me also tell you about why it's beneficial to move forward, and a win-win."

"First of all, I understand you feel like you need time. Well, I agree with you. I believe you do need more time. In fact, at my company we believe in giving our customers all the time in the world to validate their decision. What we're doing today is starting the process. In essence, Mr. Customer, what we're trying to do today is not get married, but get engaged. I'm asking you to start this process. I need time to actually get you the product, to get this done for you, to set things up before we're even ready to go. And in the meantime, you have every right to change your mind. You can push pause, or you can push stop. Any time in the next three days, you don't even have to call me—all you have to do is just text me a sad-face emoji, and I'll know you're pushing pause or stop.

"But today, I'm going to propose we get my job done, which is a win for me. And I'm going to propose a way that we can make it a win-win for both of us. Does that sound like something you'd be interested in hearing about? And here's what the proposal is: I have a huge problem, and if you can help me with that problem, I'm going to have more money in this deal. And you and I can use that money to make this a better deal for you. What everybody's worried about is that there could be a better deal, but they're too polite to bring it up. So I'm the one who is going to bring it up, Mr. Customer. I have a huge problem: it's the end of the quarter [or it's the end of the month or whatever thing is happening the day after tomorrow], and we've got this huge backlog. I've got a scheduling issue, and if you do decide it's a yes, Mr. Customer, we'll get started so you don't have to wait as long."

About 75 percent of the time, this works. They say it makes a lot of sense and are ready to get engaged. These guys have one leg to stand on, and it's that they want to do it on a different day. We're going to yank that leg right out from underneath them. And they will be happy—they will feel good about making a decision. Remember: you're still going to

194

get the 10 percent of people who cancel, and that is not a tragedy, just math. What is a tragedy is when somebody is completely sold and you didn't do the work to get them closed.

This is not a soft close. This is just pulling their crutch away. Their crutch is that they need more time, and I'm going to take that crutch away and leave them without a crutch. And this is how I do it: "Mr. Customer, the state of California makes me give you three days. I have to make you sign a piece of paper acknowledging that you have three days to validate that this is a good decision. Now, I've got to tell you, Mr. Customer, I don't really like the three-day thing because it makes you feel anxious. And I feel anxious. Is it midnight on the third day, or what? So let's do this: why don't we just cross out the three-day thing on the paperwork? And we're just going to make it 10 days. Is that enough time for you to validate the decision and move forward? Is that going to be enough time for you to talk to your accountant, to pray about it, or to do whatever you need to do?"

When you say three days, they start thinking, *OK, I got to get on the Internet now. When you leave, I'm going to be online researching.* When you say 10 days, they feel as if they have all the time in the world to get this figured out. And by that time, we will have had our happy party. Everything's good. Everything's moving along fine.

"Yes, that's enough time."

They always say that. They never say months. They always say days. They want you to be convinced that they're going solar as soon as possible. So now I'm going to bring that back and use it.

"Is it enough time? If not, I mean, I could make it 12 days. How many days? I mean, you and I are going to make an agreement, and that agreement is going to provide all the time in the world for you to validate that this was an awesome decision for you. And you can check out my ratings. You can check out my reviews. I've already told you where the pricing is going to be. If you need to validate that, feel free. I've got no concern, no issue whatsoever with you guys going out into the market during that time. But in the meantime, let me tell you what I'm going to do." And I've got my little folder with my "one more thing."

I open up this folder and put all the paperwork on the table, and I'm going to sell them this story about why they need an upgraded warranty and what it costs. And there are certain things I can't really share with you from a proprietary standpoint about my company and exactly how we do it, but I'm going to come up with a few monetary benefits that are not included in that proposal that are good for 30 days.

But we need to start the process. They'll have all the time in the world, but we're going to use that time to get the process further down the road.

Then you move into the benefits of signing today. If they do, they can make money. But it's only good for today. It's time for the "Today Only" Close:

1. "I'd like you to let us put a sign in your yard letting your neighbors know that we are your solar-installation company. By the way, for the neighbors to whom you introduce me, along with friends and family, we are going to pay you a $500 referral fee. That is not part of this offer, but it's something my company does. In fact, a third of the customers we have come from our existing customers referring us to their friends, family, and neighbors.

2. "The second thing we'd like your help with is giving us an online review on Yelp or Facebook. Are you guys on Facebook? We have hundreds and hundreds of reviews, but as you know, people are much more likely to leave a review when they're unhappy than when they're very happy. That's one of the reasons we are so proud of our 4.8-star average on Yelp and Facebook. Now, we are planning on you being a five-star review. We would love to have

your commitment to do that after the installation is complete and you're happy.

3. "Give us the names of three people you know who own a home and who we can say hello to. You don't need to call them or do anything. I will just reach out to let them know that we are working with you to get your solar installed and to see if they would like to get the information. We don't even need to tell them where we got the info if that is better. By the way, as I mentioned, we pay $500 for each referral who signs up.

4. "The last thing I would need your help with is getting this process going and getting the paperwork done tonight. As we discussed, you would still have all the time in the world, but we are both going to benefit by having my company get all of these milestones accomplished while you have that time. And this offer is our attempt to make that a no-brainer."

What is this special offer? It almost doesn't matter. It needs to have high perceived value and be a good reason for them to let go of their plan, which is to wait a few days, and instead to go with your plan, which is getting the process started today.

I like to combine a couple of items. One that has a high perceived value but no or low cost, such as an improved warranty that you were prepared to include anyway, is perfect. Point out a component of the installation that has a limited warranty, and make a big deal about what the cost is to extend that. Let that sit with them the whole presentation as something they want but don't want to pay out of pocket for. Sometimes this is enough of an incentive. If it's not (and this is a read that has to be made as you're making the offer), then remember: the bigger the system, the more incentive you may need. The second incentive is a high-appeal item like a gift card or cash rebate. I like to use a $500 cash rebate. The cost for these items can be built into the proposal pricing so that it doesn't impact the project's target margin and commissions. It also preserves margin for more significant incentives and discounts if needed later. You're going to have to work with your company to work out what you can or cannot offer.

Whatever you're giving, follow it with a closing question: "Does this seem like a reasonable plan?"

And they're going to let go because they want all this stuff. I'm going to explain to them the referrals, offering them $500 apiece. I'm going to explain this warranty thing that's going to be monumentally better. And then, of course, I'm going to write them a check for $500, and I'll explain that that's because I would rather give them that money than spend it on marketers or whatever. It just has to be a plausible story. It has to be one that you're comfortable saying, and it has to be one that you believe. And because you're not coming back, this is all true.

"This is available right now. I'm not coming back, so it's not available tomorrow. And it's not because I'm a jerk. It's not because I'm a high-pressure guy—it's because this is my job. I'm here to get my job done. If you can help me do my job, I'll be willing to improve this offer a little bit. Otherwise, I have a sales guy who I would have to employ to follow you around for the next three weeks, three months, or three years. That costs money."

If they really want to wait, you can tell them the offer is good for, say, 30 days, and when they're ready, someone else can come back and set them up. Either way, this is your last meeting with the customer. The customer thinks there's going to be another meeting, and he's going to try to get you to believe that there's going to be another meeting. You're the one in the meeting who needs to understand that this is the only meeting and that there's not going to be another meeting in at least 95 percent of cases. If you think you can prove me wrong, that's because you are returning to people who are sold but not closed. And those people could be sold and then sign up tomorrow or the next day, but they also could have been sold on the first day. And you used up another time slot with somebody who was sold because you didn't want to do the things, or you didn't know how to do the things, or you saw the things that you needed to do and then didn't do it.

The problem is that the person you're letting down is *you*. You're going to make the amount of money that you decide to make this year. The person who's getting let down in that meeting—because you bought the objection that they wanted to do it on a different day—is the customer. You were sent there to do a job, and you didn't do the job. You had the tools in your toolbox, yet you decided, "I don't want to pull those tools out."

The powerful thing about the "Today Only" Close is that you're not coming back. You have more appointments to get to, so it's a yes or a no. Don't be afraid to ask them to do it right now. Because once the salesman leaves, all the urgency goes away.

By the way, timeshare guys know the art of the "Today Only" Close. They understand that if they give a presentation in Aruba about vacation-home ownership and a customer sits through that presentation but doesn't sign up today, they're not going to call that salesman back from Cincinnati, Ohio, and say yes.

It really does cost less money to sign them up today than it does to send them back tomorrow. You know what it costs to sign them up tomorrow? Another sale. One of those three or four slots tomorrow is going to be spent trying to follow up with this guy for a meeting that doesn't happen. Am I willing to give up $500 of my commission if I can get them on paper today? Hell, yeah. Am I willing to give up double that? Hell, yeah. Some grand is better than no grand. Guess what you're getting if you have to come back? No grand. What am I getting if I can sign them up with a $500 or $750 cash rebate today or whatever it is that they happen to want? It really does cost more money for me to come back three days from now and take one of those appointments off my calendar, one where I was going to be with someone brand new and have another opportunity to close. It adds up to quite a bit.

An objection is just a request for more information so that they can make a different decision or make sure they're making the right decision. They've decided not to commit today so they can have more time. But it has to be today. You need to find a way that it has to be today. You need your no or your yes and nothing in between.

That's all it takes. And if they don't say yes, then you've got a no, which is what you came there to get anyway. And what you didn't leave with was an invitation to follow them around like a pathetic little kid for the next three weeks, three months, or three years.

Let's review the components of the "Today Only" Close:
1. Review everything you've gone over with them and have them agree that this makes sense;
2. Let them know they have all the time in the world;
3. Offer an exchange of value, not a discount; and
4. Ask the actual closing question

Let me go deeper into the last one because the exact words are not as important as you being comfortable with saying them:

Does this sound good?
Does this make sense? Would you like to give it a try?
It really seems that this idea appeals to you. Am I right about that?
Can I just get a copy of your driver's license to get the paperwork started? (The assumptive closing question.)
Does this seem like a reasonable plan?

Practice these questions in the mirror, in the car, or with your fellow closers, and get super comfortable saying them so you can push through the nervousness that inevitably comes at that moment.

Ask one of these questions and then shut up. The next side to talk loses. I once asked one of these questions and then calmly sat and watched my customers look at each other for more than a minute. I am the one guy who does not say a word for several minutes. I badly want to say one more thing but remember that the next one to talk loses. I am patiently waiting for them to say, "Yes, that sounds reasonable. What's the next step?"

The Best Close is the One That Has Not Been Invented Yet
This close does not work every single time. But it works most of the time.

But let's say you did all that and they say, "We still want to think about it." Now what? Are we done? Are we ready to take no for an answer? Hell no, we're not even close. We're several no's away. Now it's time to empty the clip. What do you have to lose at this point? You literally have nothing to lose because now you use the hammer.

You've made it awkward. You haven't preserved the rapport, so they're not going to like you tomorrow anyway. You've still got a double-digit-percentage success rate of turning this thing into signed paperwork today. But if you leave, it's going to go down, just half a percent, 1 percent, 2 percent—not enough to count. You have literally nothing to lose. And you're still at the kitchen table; they've not thrown you out yet. Do you know how many kitchens I've been thrown out of? None.

It doesn't get that awkward. You're afraid that it's going to get that awkward, but it never, ever, ever gets that awkward. But at some point, when somebody really convinces me that this isn't happening, then I know that I'm done. But that's why I'm there, sometimes three and a half hours later. Because if they haven't asked me to leave and they haven't bought, then we're not done. We still have stuff to talk about.

So one of my favorite empty-the-clip closes is the "If I could, would you?"

"Understand, Mr. Customer, this was my best offer. That's all I got. I really want your business. I'm here. You're here. Why don't you put me to work? I know the owner of the company. I see him every single day. He's on the other side of this phone call. We want your business. He wants your business. We're trying to hit this goal for the month. I kind of think you're in a spot where we might be able to talk him into doing something crazy. If I could get them to do something crazy, would you want me to call him?"

"What are we talking about?"

"Well, I don't know. I just showed you this rebate of X dollars. If I were able to get him to go berserk and double the rebate—I don't even know how we pay for that—but if I got him to double the rebate, if I could get him to say yes to that, would we have a deal? If I could, would you?"

Once you've gotten to this point, don't you dare offer them anything else without saying this: "If I could get this approved, if I can talk my manager into this, would we then have a deal?" That's the "If I could, would you?"

If they say, "Yeah, then we'd have a deal," now we've got something to work for. Maybe we're really talking price, so get those deals out of the customer. Ask what you have to do. Make a big show of calling your boss (or the owner or your good friend) and going through an elaborate conversation about why this would be a terrific new addition to our customer list and our installations in the neighborhood. Talk him into it and get him to say yes. Then get off the phone with a big smile and say, "Great news, Bob and Judy!" Go in for a big handshake with one of them and say, "He agreed to your offer and we have a deal! Congratulations, you are going solar. I know we've been here for a while. It will take just a few minutes to get the paperwork done. Do either of you have a copy of your driver's license for the paperwork?"

Do not give up. They say that necessity is the mother of invention, and the best closes are the ones that have not been invented yet. It's the one that this customer needs to bring him across the finish line. Remember, this is a contest of wills. If you continue this process in a good-natured way and keep it positive but continue driving towards the finish line, you will be surprised by how often the customer will see the finish line ahead as well and join you in the desire to get across it for a win-win.

The Hammer
Grab the hammer, hit the nail on the head, and just see what happens. I don't know why it works. I just know the guys who had sold aluminum siding told me 30 years ago it would work, and they were right. People are just afraid it will make things awkward to get out the hammer. Well, YouTube videos never make the situation awkward, and that's why we're not sending a YouTube video to make a sale. You're there to make it awkward. Except that if they do buy, it won't be awkward—it will be a joyous occasion.

People who try to preserve the rapport don't realize there ain't that much rapport there anyway. How much real rapport do you have with someone after an hour? How much of a relationship are you really risking? And since you and I both know there's not going to be another meeting, it really doesn't matter anyway.

You're at a point where you have absolutely nothing to lose and everything to gain. If, at that moment, you refuse to buy the customer's objection and decide you're going to sell rather than be sold, you're going to be better off; more importantly, you're going to be serving the customer. If they're at all interested but you don't close, someone else will.

I was sent here to do a job. It's a lot more important for me to do it than not. As a professional salesperson, I have a service. My service to you is to help you understand that you should be looking at my product, and then I'm going to help you. I'm not going to convince you. I'm going to help you understand that you're better off by moving forward today than you are by moving forward tomorrow. That's the service we provide.

You're not going to change their mind. You're going to make them a different offer and they're going to make a different decision. You've got to get them to completely dump out all their objections and all their concerns on the initial proposal. Narrow it down and ask them to buy again. "Is this making sense? Have you heard enough to move forward today?"

When they want to think about it, you have to pull the hammer out of the bag and hit the nail on the head. It's going to make the situation awkward, so you have to overcome that concern and fear.

But there's another reason I haven't said for why you aren't pulling the hammer out. And the reason is because you are buying the objection that they really do need more time, that they need to do this on a day that's not today. Somehow, magically, between now and that day, they're going to have more information? No. And if they have more information, it's because they now have 75 sales guys and one of them is going to be a better closer than you, and he's getting the business, not you. So if you really believe that there's going to be this process between now and next Friday that ends with them really prepared to make a decision, you are the one that's going to be sorely disappointed.

Let's say a customer tells you: "Man, you're awesome. You're my guy. This is great, and there is zero chance I'm not going to buy." I will always take the bet that they'll ghost you or make an excuse for another day. I don't even need to know the person or what was said. If it's not today, it's more than likely not going to happen. And you will be the sucker for believing it, every time.

There's a difference between an objection and a condition. An objection is a reason that you can overcome: it costs too much, I need to talk to my wife, something that is flimsy. A condition is a real barrier, such as:

they're bankrupt. Then it's over. But an objection? You just keep going until you get those three no's.

The 1, 2, 3's of Referrals

I've talked a little about offering rewards for referrals to help you close, which really does work, but I want to say more about how referrals are incredibly valuable in and of themselves. The most valuable lead prospect you can possibly identify is a referral from somebody who has bought from you already. And, as you can see from what we've just covered, the best time to mine for referrals is while you're still selling the original customer. I do this with my "1, 2, 3."

Every single sales process that I have when I go to move into the close if they don't jump onto the boat is asking for help by making them an offer where they can get money from referrals. I say, "You know, that offer is in your email, and it's good for 30 days. Now, I want to talk to you about another offer. And if you can help me out with something, I want to make that a win-win and make you a much better offer. The first thing I want to ask of you is to put a sign in your yard to get us some exposure. The second is to write us a review on Yelp or Facebook. So that's one and two. The third is to give me three names I can reach out to. I just want the names of three people. Your mom, your brother, and that guy at work. Part of my offer—whether it's the discount, the rebate, the incentive, the whatever that I'm about to offer them—is for you to give me three names. And you don't have to give me the numbers, just the names of three people, and we can work together at a later date and see if we can turn some of those people into referrals. And if we can, you're going to get $500 for each one of these. And by the way, that list has space for 10 names (I have a pre-printed list for this). So maybe we can really go to work figuring this out and find 10 people to follow up with, and if we can, that's $5,000 for you."

And this is now a condition of the other offer I'm making. When I'm in that process of seeing if they can help me with "1, 2, 3," they know at the end that I'm going to offer them something, and they are ready for it.

By the way, getting the names is a sort of mini-habit. You're not pushing for a number or bona fide referral—just the names. Low bar.

A lot of people almost never give the names, but there are some people who get really excited. I once had a lady who really got going. She said to me, "You know, I could tell Marge about this. And we could talk to the neighbors about this. I really want to get six people to do this because I'm going on an Alaska cruise in September, and I really want to take my sister with me, but it's going to cost $3,000."

I said, "Wow, that's really fascinating. That's a great idea, what a great goal. I tell you what, let's do this: you get me six people, that'll pay you $3,000, and I'm going to chip in another $1,000."

She followed up with them, and I eventually ended up with their phone numbers. I sold six of her referrals, and she got a check for $4,000. I've never been happier to give somebody a check. As it turns out, she was the front-office lady at a grammar school, and you could not get by her without her asking if you had gone solar.

I can also do a similar referral incentive if I've already gotten the sale. I have them walk me to the door (they always walk you to the door), and as they do, I ask them to step out onto the porch and do me a favor.

I ask, "Which of your neighbors around you are you guys friendly with? You know, who do you guys have barbecues with? Who are the good people on the street? Who are the people that you like?"

And they'll point them out: "Oh, those are the Johnsons, and we definitely barbecue with them. But we're really super-good friends with the Smiths. We've been on vacation with them a couple times. Don't under any circumstances talk to that guy—he's the one that reports everybody to the HOA any time a weed pops up."

I have them tell me the names of all the people in the neighborhood with whom they have a relationship. And as I'm writing them down, I tell them I'm going to put those people on their list.

I say, "Remember when I told you about the $500 referral fee? I'm going to put them on your list."

Afterwards, I'll walk down the driveway to knock on those doors. Those people are most often the ones who say yes because I'll go to these new prospects and talk about my new friends who I just sold to.

"You know the Joneses, the guys you have barbecues with? Anyway, they're going solar, we just got their design together, and all the paperwork is done. Just wanted to say hello. Here's my card."

And then I'm going to have the conversation that I have with people at their door, and I'm going to close them for an appointment right now. And if I get that appointment, I'm going to walk right back over to the first customer's house, knock on their door, and say, "Good news! I just talked to the folks you have barbecues with, and they're having me over on Tuesday to show them a solo presentation. Once I get to this point, a lot of folks sign up. So hopefully they talk to you between now and then, and I'll meet with them Tuesday. If they sign up, you guys are getting $500. Who else do you know on the street?" When you tell someone they're now really getting $500, that gets them going.

Here's another technique: when the system gets installed, I'm going to come back and say, "Mr. Customer, every time we install a system, we do a lot of marketing in the neighborhood because everybody's curious about solar, and they saw your system go up on the roof. And now is the best time for us to hit them up and ask them if they'd like to see a presentation. So we're about to mail everybody a thing. I've got a kid who's going to run up and down the street and hang a door hanger on everybody's door. I'm probably going to go knock on those doors. But I wanted to talk to you because—do you remember that $500 referral fee we talked about? Well, I want to make sure we don't steal your referrals. So tell me who I should reach out to right away so that they don't get swept up in our marketing and you don't lose out on the referral. So step out onto the porch with me here. Talk to me about this neighbor, that neighbor, that neighbor, that neighbor, this neighbor, that neighbor—the ones you're at the country club with, you know, who you play tennis with. Who is someone I should put onto your list?"

And now I'm really putting them into a bind. They either cough up the names or they get robbed.

Another way of getting referrals is to give them my training class called "Do not give out my business card." Basically, I'll give them a couple of business cards but then tell them to promise me not to give it to anyone they think might be interested. It's meant to be confusing. When two people talk about a product they like and one of them hands the other a business card, the person who takes the business card almost never calls. So I always ask them not to give out my business card. And then this is the key to them earning the referral and me earning the sale:

"Mr. Customer, as you're talking about having gone solar and someone's interested in talking to you, it's important not to give them my card or my number, because they're never, almost never going to call. They say they're going to call, but they don't call. So here's what you do: you tell them that you're working with the greatest solar guy on the planet. Because I'm the owner, tell them you're working with the owner of the company, and he's in three or four of these meetings every day so he's impossible to get a hold of. But you want them to work with me instead of being assigned to the sales department. So here's what I'm going to do: I'm going to text him right now, and I'm going to have him reach out to you. You text me that person's phone number, and I'm going to call them in the next 24 hours."

And I am going to be much, much more effective at getting them to agree to set up an appointment for me to come and show them the information. In fact, I'm going to be phenomenal at it because that's what I do. They're not going to be very good at motivating someone to call me—it's just very rare.

Not everyone is comfortable giving out their friends' numbers for referrals, so this is an excellent way for them to still get referrals. But if they do give me a number, I say something like, "Mr. Customer, since you know I'm in meetings all day, what I do is I hit this little auto-reply that says, 'I'm sorry, but I'm in a meeting. I'm going to call you after the meeting.' But you know what? I want to put your friend into my phone so that when he calls, I'll know it's him. And I'll step out of the meeting that I'm in, and I'll take his call. What's his telephone number? Awesome. I've got him here in my phone. I'm going to be looking out for his call. By the way, Mr. Customer, if I haven't heard from him in a couple of days, I'll go ahead and reach out to him. Does that make sense?"

Now I'm getting his permission. Because even if they insist they'll have their friends call me, nine times out of ten they won't.

Remember: You're Not Coming Back!

Let's come back to the frame and summarize. We built this frame for a reason, and we are about to put it to work. Its purpose is to introduce and make real the following sentence: "I'm not coming back." The frame was to hold the door. In the presentation, we built the door. We are now going to close the door.

What the frame accomplishes is to eliminate all other options in a way that is not about pressure and is not offensive. It is just a fact. You can also think of this as a corral that you are driving the herd into. The prospect thinks that you are a salesman and are desperate for a sale. They think that you will do anything and waste any amount of time doing it their way. That you have all the time in the world and will be happy to chase them around for weeks or months to have this signing party on a different day.

We construct a frame that takes this away from them—and does so in such a way that it is not your fault. In the very beginning, you told them your job: "My job is to meet with three or four new customers every day. This time of year, we are so busy that I literally do that six or seven days a week. [This is true for me, and if you implement what you learn in this book, it will be true for you as well.] It's my job to explain the three big elements that make this worth it to you, to show you how it can work for your life, and answer all of your questions. That's it. Now, if I have done my job, you will have been educated to the point where you know whether this strategy is for you. It is not for everybody. If this is making a lot of sense and the numbers look great, it is also my job to help you get the process started today, get the paperwork going, and get my installation department working on your project. This won't happen overnight. It takes my company a number of weeks to get this on your roof. There is absolutely nothing that you have to do, and we will make sure you have all the time in the world to be 100-percent sure this is the right thing for your family while we get the project started.

"If this is not making sense or you need more time, that is no problem. I am going to leave the design proposal with all the numbers with you, and those numbers will be good for 30 days. My follow-up department will be sure we are there when you're ready. Fair enough?"

What we have just communicated is that I am not able to come back. What I do as an expert and a consultant is very specific, and my time is very valuable. This comes out in my story and in building the frame. And it is true. My time is too valuable to chase one out of ten shots, and I do meet with brand-new customers every day. Make that your story. I am not being a jerk to say that I won't come back. I am telling them what my job is and that I am not able to come back. I am not in the "come back" department—and neither are you.

Part 6

Following Up and a Call to Action

Chapter 18
The 7-Figure Follow Up

I believe that if you single-mindedly pursue the close in the meeting and use the tools outlined in this book, your follow-up game may not produce the same results as some of your competitors and associates who are basically planting seeds and tending the fields as a farmer. In fact, depending on how awkward it got while trying to help the customer make a decision, there may not be a lot of rapport left between you. I like to joke that if a customer doesn't sign up and buy from me on the night of the appointment, there's a good chance I'm not really welcome back.

Let's face it: if you have really done absolutely everything you can think of to try to help the customer cross the threshold, the walk to the door after you've really packed up may not be a merry occasion. That is the primary reason many salespeople do not reach into the closing toolbox. They believe that if they preserve the rapport that they have spent hours building, they will have a greater chance of closing on a day in the future—hopefully in the near future. This may be the case, but in my experience, if you are skilled at using the master-closing techniques, the people who will buy on a different day make up literally a single-digit percentage of the population.

Having said that, I have learned that a positive, proactive approach to following up with customers using several media all at once can be very compelling, and I have learned it is quite effective. And so, when all else fails, build a bridge to a seven-figure follow-up process.

The seven-figure follow-up is going to have two different categories: the people who buy and get on the boat and the people who stay ashore.

Most salespeople think follow-up is all about the people who didn't buy. They are wasting a tremendous amount of time dealing with the people who didn't buy because they probably never will buy. I'm going to put them in the 5-percent category and devote about 5-percent of my time to following up with them. If someone doesn't buy or says no at the door, what needs to be going through your head is: *Some will, some won't. So what? Who's next?*

When a lion goes after an antelope, gives it everything she can, and leaves her mark on the hindquarters of that animal but misses the kill, she goes hungry that night. When hunting the next day, does she track the antelope she missed yesterday? No, she stalks the herd and selects the animal that appears to be the most likely successful kill. In fact, if she does come across the one she marked, she may pass it by thinking that one may be tougher than some of the others.

One reason it just doesn't work very well is because there's heat and passion when you are there. The iron is hot! After you walk out the door, that iron gets cold within minutes. And if you keep going back and beating on this cold iron, you're going to get some of them, but it's literally going to be a single digit percentage of them. Maybe they don't like me or I'm not the right guy for them. I'm not helping them make that decision, and I'm certainly not doing so by pestering them on the phone. They'll take your first call and come up with some reason as to why they are still not ready. The next call, they don't take. By the time you've called them three or four times, they've blocked your call, which is really demoralizing. You thought you had this great relationship. You preserved this great rapport to use on a different day, and it never happens.

If you're a farmer and you cultivate all these relationships as if you're cultivating seeds, then those relationships will mature at different rates, right? I know salespeople who do this, and they're quite good at it. But I would contend that a large percentage of those people could have been signed up the first day. And they're not signing them up. Instead, they're putting them in their little farm, and then they're farming and farming and farming. That's a different book. I don't know how to write that book. I'm not the guy to consult if you want to find out how to be a better farmer. I'm a terrible farmer.

I believe it's much more important to follow up with the people who did buy. I start the referral conversation at the end of the initial sale with a little training class. I let them know I am interested not just in saving them money but also in making them a lot of money. They are basically now a solar franchise. Everyone they know from now on who owns a home is going to be going solar eventually, and they might as well do that as your referral.

I email every single customer who has ever bought from me, including all the new ones. I tell them about a promotion that I'm running. I always have the $500 referral fee, but this month (or this quarter or for the next two weeks), anyone who reaches out to me with a successful referral (one that I get signed up) will get a bonus. I will offer anyone who gets two referrals in the next two weeks one additional referral fee. The email subject will say "Make $1,500 in the next 14 days."

I use email to follow up with people who are too scared to pull the trigger and don't want to make decisions. I have two bins through which I'll distribute mass emails, in addition to my promotional emails to people I've already closed:

TBC (To Be Closed): they may be ready someday. Call me when it hurts.

TBR (To Be Rescheduled): people who set an appointment and needed to reschedule

I try not to spend a lot of time on them, but I'll send them regular drip emails. And when they decide that they've somehow ended up in the zone they were waiting for and they're now ready to pull the trigger, they will have received an email from me sometime in the last four weeks. I will also use outbound telemarketers to periodically call these lists and find the people who are now ready.

My favorite follow-up is with what I call green pins. When one of my setters or I have a great conversation at the door with a prospect but they absolutely will not set an appointment, we will mark them in our canvassing app with a green pin. They are also called "strong-lead callbacks." When someone does that, we try to close for an email address and a phone number since they won't set an appointment. "I'll tell you what: since you're going to do research, let me send you some information. What's the best email address to send that to? And what's the best cell-phone number to follow up with you?" We have a lot of fun finishing every team sales meeting with a strong-lead-callback session. We will call these leads live on speakerphone to do a door pitch over the phone and try to set the appointment. It's great training, and we almost always get at least one, if not several, appointments. That's a great way to make money while in a sales meeting.

Chapter 19
Final Words and Resources

My sustained success in solar started out with reading two pages a day of Stephen Guise's book *Mini Habits*. Throughout my life, I have read about one-third of hundreds of sales and personal-development books without finishing one of them. Then I heard about *Mini-Habits*, and the first prescribed habit of reading two pages per day led me to finish my first ever nonfiction book.

The key to understanding habits is to comprehend that people do not rise to the level of their goals; they fall to the level of their habits. Every few days, everybody falls. You get inspired, motivated, disciplined for a few days, and then you fall again. The trick Is to use that inspiration and motivation to build habits that will only let you fall so far before you take one single positive step forward.

I have been greatly influenced by the book *Think and Grow Rich* by Napoleon Hill. Hill wrote a variety of books over his lifetime, but he was actually changed by Andrew Carnegie, a steel magnate who was kind of the Bill Gates of his time. Carnegie had cornered the steel market and acquired a fortune that, in inflation-adjusted terms, made him a billionaire and one of the richest men in the world. Napoleon Hill interviewed him.

In the book, Hill explains that the biggest thing successful people have in common is a certain mindset. It's about explaining to your brain that it has a job, which is to think and grow rich. That requires a whole bunch of things: discipline, creativity, imagination, diligence, the ability to harness the energies of many people. These fundamental concepts all start with having a chief purpose. If you dedicate yourself to that purpose and program your brain to focus on and work diligently at it, then your brain will respond. If you don't give your brain a job to do, it runs around like a puppy: anxious, distracted, spinning.

So I created the regimen of reading two pages a day of *Mini Habits* and of *Think and Grow Rich*. After that, I did it with the other books that Napoleon Hill wrote.

Several years ago, I joined the D2DExperts Circle mastermind, which is a group of owners and CEOs who run door-to-door companies. Among other things, we read a book every month. Many of those books have helped me, but the one that took my game to a completely different level was *The Miracle Morning* by Hal Elrod. The idea is to start your day one hour earlier and to use that one hour to do a very specific set of habits. I had the opportunity to meet Hal and listen to him share. There are so many things that are impressive about his story, but none more so than his breakthrough from mediocrity to the top-selling salesperson at Cutco, the knife manufacturer. He relates nearly failing as a salesman before turning his career around using advice from his manager. His manager urges him to make an unbreakable commitment to making 10 calls to prospects in the morning and then another 10 calls in the afternoon. He shares that his breakthrough came when he realized that the most important thing about those 10 calls was to have them be done and over with. It didn't matter that he approached the calls with that approach; he consistently made the appointments he needed to climb to the top of a company renowned for its sales acumen. The main prescription of *The Miracle Morning* is to start your day one hour earlier and to use that one hour to do a very specific set of habits. The commitment requires enduring about 10 days of those habits feeling unbearable, but after the 30th day you will experience the feeling of being unstoppable.

I had the great pleasure of meeting Tim Grover when he was the keynote speaker at the 2019 D2DCon. His talk inspired me and several others to start the morning-accountability call every day no matter what. Tim Grover refers to super-elite athletes like Michael Jordan and Kobe Bryant as "cleaners." For the first couple of years, we called the meeting the Cleaner's Club and kicked it off every day the way we still do today, which is to read a few paragraphs of one of his books. At first, we read his first book, *Relentless,* and currently we're reading his outstanding book *Winning.* His straightforward, no-bullshit approach to confronting the way most of us think and contrasting that with how multiple championship winners think cuts right to the heart of the issue every day.

I've been clean and sober with alcohol and drugs for over 38 years. Without the help of several twelve-step programs and my higher power, I am absolutely sure that I would have had a life that would've led no one to suggest that I write a book. I have no doubt that I would have a story filled with calamity and misery. I count my blessings every day that I found sobriety when I did and that I've been able to build a life that I am proud of and enjoy by living without alcohol and drugs one day at a time.

The original title of this book was going to be *Get One No.* It expressed the idea of overcoming inertia and finding momentum by going from zero doors to one door, using the idea that you're just going to get someone to say no. It is hard to understate how brutal it is to deal with that inertia. It is a plague upon people who make a living going door to door. I have not found a way to lessen it or make it go away. In fact, I believe it gets worse and worse over time. On the cover of this book, the word "no" has the sun shining through it, which suggests that all of the power and energy to succeed at what we do comes through that one word of rejection. I teach people to embrace it, monetize it, and use No Matter

Watt habits to break through that inertia to the extraordinary rewards that wait on the other side of a door. The strangely high pay that comes as a result is due to the fact that 99 percent of people won't compete with them because of their abhorrent reaction to voluntarily experiencing rejection.

I participated in a retreat with Sharon Lechter, the co-author of *Rich Dad Poor Dad*. We were talking about how I'd been able to use the principles that had led to success with sobriety in my sales career. I was talking about how the old-timers would tell newcomers to go to 90 meetings in 90 days—even if your ass falls off. If it falls off, pick it up and take it to a meeting. She seized upon the connection and said, "That's it!" That is your true message, and it should be the title of the book.

Early in my sales career in the 1980s and 1990s, I was very fortunate to attend several sales seminars by the great Tom Hopkins. His training set me on the path to being a successful career salesman. I had the great fortune to share a stage with him at an industry conference called Knockstar 2. It was very exciting to hear him tell a story I heard him share from the stage many years before about being dragged out of the real-estate office, which had no customers in it, and into the neighborhood, which was full of people who own homes. He shared about the absolute dread of going up to a door and about the insecurity of not knowing what to say once he was there. He related the story of going up to a home and having the man of the house ask him if he had a real-estate license, to which Tom replied yes. The man then yelled for his wife to come to the door, and she asked him again, "Do you have a real-estate license?" Of course, once again he said yes. The couple embraced each other and invited Tom to their kitchen table. They shared with him that they were quite anxious about the gentleman being reassigned to a different city with his company and that he would have to leave her alone there to sell the house. The two of them had prayed together the night before that they would be sent a licensed real-estate agent to help them with the transition. Tom realized that instead of being afraid of what somebody would say to him at the door, he just needed to find the people to whom he was the answer to a prayer.

I've had a successful sales career for decades—the type of success that keeps you employed at your company and near the top of a leaderboard, making the kind of income you can use to pay your bills and then some. I performed at that level for literally decades, but it was far below my potential. And then I happen to be in the right place at the right time. It was a test of comfort to leave a salaried position. I had a six-figure salary, and I needed to prove to myself that I could replace that in more of an entrepreneurial undertaking with solar. Initially, I was really spurred on by the pressure that comes from that, and I did pretty well. But I soon got back to a merely acceptable level of performance.

Then this deadline for a solar rebate came into being, and I realized that I was going to have this opportunity to show customers an opportunity that was disappearing. It was called net metering, and it was going to be gone by a certain date. I realized my opportunity, and my customers' opportunity, was here today and not tomorrow. It occurred to me that if I could work this hard and sell two or three of these in a week, why wouldn't I? So that's what I started to do. I was just responding to an opportunity, which got me working at a different level—and I was having much, much different results.

Everything I've learned since then, and everything I do now, is what I've taught you in this book. Whether you're trying just to be comfortable or you're looking to earn seven figures, the advice I give will get you to whatever level you want to reach.

I have been on dozens of podcasts talking about the subjects in this book. You can find most of those in my Instagram and Facebook posts by following me at Michael O'Donnell Sales.

Well, this book is meant to be comprehensive, but it barely scratches the surface of the context and details that we could cover in a one-on-one session. I've had the great privilege to work with Brad Lea and his Light-speed VT system to create an extensive, virtualized one-on-one training program. It can be found at www.MODSalesAcademy.com

I provide live coaching every weekday via Zoom from 8 am to 8:30 am in my "No Matter Watt Club." This coaching focuses on inspiration, accountability, and support. You would think that a job that requires no education, credentials, or experience and is extremely lucrative would not need a support group. However, in my experience, door-to-door sales can be extremely brutal on your state of mind, and having a group that supports you and holds you accountable can make the difference between astounding success and ending up in the weeds. I have a burning desire to make this coaching available to anyone, so I offer it for $67 a month. You can sign up for that coaching at www.MODSalesAcademy.com

In addition I provide live training via Zoom every week. The current schedule is every Wednesday from 9 am to 10:30 am Pacific Standard time. This is included in the live coaching.

As of 2022 there have been approximately 3 million rooftop solar systems installed in the United States to date. At the beginning of the Biden administration, the United States rejoined the Paris Climate Accord and made a public commitment to reducing our carbon emissions by half by the end of the decade. If we want to meet these ambitious goals, we will need to multiply the number of solar systems installed tenfold, reaching 30 million households. At the same time, many Americans will find that the income they are earning at their current job will no longer provide the lifestyle it had in the past. I believe that this tremendous challenge will meet an army of individuals who are looking to find a way to multiply their income while doing something meaningful for their family, their community, and the planet. If you find yourself wondering if you have what it takes to generate a high six-figure income, perhaps even a seven-figure income, helping families come to come to the conclusion that they are ready to switch from destructive carbon-fuel homes to clean, green, renewable homes, I hope you will reach out to me to discuss putting you to work at SunSolar Solutions. Together I believe we can succeed in this great endeavor. You can connect with me directly by emailing me at michael@sunsolarsolutions.com.

BIBLIOGRAPHY

Guise, Stephen.
Mini Habits. Selective Entertainment LLC, 2013.

Guise, Stephen.
Mini Habits for Weight Loss. Selective Entertainment LLC, 2016.

Guise, Stephen.
Elastic Habits. Selective Entertainment LLC, 2019.

Hill, Napoleon.
Think and Grow Rich. The Ralston Society, 1937.

Mandino, Og.
Greatest Salesmen in the World. Bantam Books, 1968.

Ziegler, Zig.
See You At the Top

Grover, Tim.
Relentless and WINNING

Hopkins, Tom.
Master the Art of Selling

Made in the USA
Monee, IL
07 August 2023

40586174R00122